Alchemy

~

the completely transformative
power of love and joy

What People Are Saying About *Alchemy*

"I feel so happy and excited today. Like the others, this is not the first step on my journey. But, I believe, this step is the most important. *Why?* Because you have given me the tools to find and work with what I want. I have read books that said simply stop the negative thoughts. Okay. Meditate. Okay. But then what? (A favorite university professor once told me, 'When all you have is a hammer, everything looks like a nail.') I now have a resplendent toolbox." —Judith, Ottawa, Ontario

"Thank you for the wonderful book. I started to read it last night and could not believe the insights it brought. I plan on giving your website details out to all of my meditation students. I am certain that it will prove extremely helpful to them.—Steve Sonnefeld, Philadelphia, Pennsylvania

"I've just had a session with Cindy. It is wondrous how quickly my experience has changed. From feeling sad, hopeless, discouraged and lost to feeling incredible peace, present, calm and a quiet joy that is expansive—expanding as I now speak about it. :) This is a magical switch! This practice has literally switched the track I was on to experiencing and wanting more and more joy!

The most important gift in my doing this practice of *Alchemy*, which is quick and simple (but wow!) is that it experientially revealed how my negative beliefs were just negative thoughts I believed!! And it was the believing of them that made me feel so bad. But they were just thoughts and they could be dropped!!! And in dropping them instantly their power dissolved, and so did my sadness. In fact I was laughing from how easy the relief was, and also from the illusion being revealed of how truly unfounded those thoughts were that I was so fervently believing!"

—Nicole, Ottawa, Ontario

"Cindy, thanks so much for your book! You have taken what was for me a life-long journey to find peace and happiness and put it all into one book.

You have truly found what Jesus meant when he said 'the kingdom of Heaven is within.' You and your work are critical as we come into the next stage of human evolution.

I have passed your book on to loved ones who have also been dramatically changed. God Bless you in all your endeavors.

I'm still following you on Twitter which is where I discovered your book, your daily reminders are a great help to stop and feel the awesome presence of Joy within." —Bruce Black, USA

"Your book is so good…it's a breakthrough for me! A real breakthrough, I will read it over and over again because something clicked when I read this and I know that it's the key that I was missing. This element that I was missing—every page, 'yes, yes, yes, she's right.'

I've been practicing law of attraction for four years now, but it seems that you gave me the key to my happiness, and I know that I will achieve it. I understand it, I can practice it, and I know it works. You made a big difference in my life just by reading your book. Thank-you!"

—Christine, Ottawa, Ontario

"I found the insights shared in your book to be deeply profound. At a time when I'm at something of a crossroads in my life, your practice really spoke to me about freeing myself from the past, from the unnecessary things I've allowed to block myself along the way. Your own experiences were very inspiring, and I'm grateful you chose to share them, and the realizations you had from them.

Your book has given me a lot of excellent ideas, and a lot of things to take to heart. I cannot wait to make them a regular part of my daily practice. Thank you so much, again, for sharing this book with me."

—Lisa Maxham Purefoy, San Jose, California

"Thank you, Cindy, for our talk today. I had this knowledge that I tend to live in my head. I have been working on being present, in the moment, and remembering to breathe. Using yoga, Reiki, and meditation, I have had glimpses of how this feels. None so powerful as the time I had to speak with you this morning. I could truly feel the difference between being constricted by my thoughts and the expansiveness of being joyfully in my body.

It is amazing to think we have this power and the ability to easily access and sustain it. What really blows me away is the timing of our call. The guilt, sadness, and disapproval I felt over giving up my dog was fresh and sudden. To be able to process that with you lifted my energy in a powerful exciting way. I am thankful for this new awareness. I look forward to continuing to grow, share, and practice this blessed gift."

—Lisa Walls

"After we hung up the phone, I rejoiced and celebrated in this wonderful realization and another one came along which made me laugh (busted once again!). If I cannot celebrate who I am then it is difficult to celebrate who others are. I thought to myself, 'I really love the part where I thought my friend should do it for me.' I can now celebrate not only who I am but also who others are, this is what makes me very happy. I am back to being present, feeling joyful and ecstatic. This truly is alchemy. Love and gratitude."—Christine xox

"Cindy, thank you so much for sharing your beautifully simplistic and powerful ways to truly shift yourself/attitude through awareness. The tools you shared with my husband and myself are a treasured gift that we will put into practice by asking those few questions to get us back into wholeness and love. Although we initially called about our daughter, you helped us to realize the importance of not just holding the space for her, but ultimately taking responsibility for only our OWN selves. May the work you do be blessed. Thank you once more. Full of gratitude."
—Veronica and Zeke Rios, USA

"Thank you so much for the wonderful session and sharing your amazing insights and wisdom with me. I LOVED IT! I felt like I was talking to a long lost friend and you made so many things clearer for me. The simplicity of your work and the way you explain it is just great but the impact of it is (was) very powerful. I loved how you would catch me and show me by using your questions how to see the truth in every experience. Blessings and love."—Sharon

"There was an "aha" moment when I understood some wise words of yours. I fell into how it would feel to have what I wanted. I accessed it and yet nothing had changed in my world other than allowing myself to have it. I have the power! I still access that feeling as I sit here typing, and it is sweet indeed! Thank you Cindy for your spiritual wisdom, for the simplicity and practicality of your wonderful technique, for your generosity, and for your God-filled laughter. May you continue to be blessed and be a blessing in all you do. With the Love we are."—Katherine Owen

"I have only had fleeting moments of inexpressible joy. Actually only two I remember really clearly. You give me hope! I have read Hicks & similar books, love them all. Yes, conscious control was what was lacking in me, has taken me 60 years to learn this is possible! I have Tolle's books too. Your book has simplified it for me, or should I say—crystallized it for me. Yes you are absolutely right I often limit my own joy, put a lid on it! Silly me! I am constantly searching for answers and your answers are the clearest I have encountered." —@GeorgeArtz, via Twitter

"Thank you for the session today Cindy. I've been searching for a way out of my old patterns of fear and pain and sadness. And yet it's amazing how locked in I have been to those feelings. I'm looking forward to putting this new shift in attention/awareness into action. Thank you for so generously giving of your time and your spirit. Namaste."—Kathryn

"What a GIFT, What a GIFT, What a Gift, these were the words I got after getting off the phone with you today, Cindy. I am now feeling Love, Joy and Happiness and some tears of JOY. I had no idea what to expect with the phone session but it was like sharing with my best friend, some personal grief issues. Which quickly disappeared with a few short questions to my body. It was a magical experience. Cindy's book was a healing experience and I can't wait for her next books to come out.

Congratulations Cindy on your winning book and sharing your personal experience and healing with the world. Many blessings."
—Wilda Hicks, Ottawa, Ontario

"Cindy, thank you so much for opening your home and soul. You're an amazing leader and teacher. I have my joy back! I have not stopped smiling or feeling so *good*. Words fail me to express what my body and mind is saying.

I want to write you a song, a poem, a dance and show you a rainbow. LoL Because you gave me the way to get out of the ebb and stay in the flow! The lessons I learned in those few but "extended" hours of loving conversation I'll cherish. And use. And share. Thank you. Namaste, sweet love." —Michelle De Angelis, Ottawa, Ontario

"They say that 'when the student is ready, the teacher appears.' This was definitely one of those times. Thank you."
—@SleepingTyger, via Twitter

"Just having finally met you elevated my 'energy' and I am on a 'rush'… you know the feeling when a long searched for puzzle piece is found and entered into the 'waiting opening'!!

Thank you so much my 'little bundle of JOY," you certainly 'walk the talk' and I will practice, practice, practice. By the way here is what my friend from Vancouver wrote to me last night…about the book:"—I. A., Ottawa, Ontario

"Thanks so much for sending the book.…I just read it and I'm tingling from head to toe. This is so IT! And the crazy thing is—I get it! And even better, I am BEING it!"
—J. Myers, Vancouver, British Columbia

"I found your book two days ago. What you have written is truly profound and really resonated with me. I was caught in a traffic jam this morning, and I decided to put the method to practice and in no time I was feeling the joy of having a fast and unobstructed ride down the highway even though I was moving at a turtle pace.

Thank you so much for sharing this wonderful gift with the whole World (I am half way around the world in Singapore)."
—Tan Teong Hin, Singapore

"I was your father two years ago! The only difference is I didn't die. I just wanted to, but I couldn't finish the job, even in the drunken, depressed, hopeless state I was in.

I was gradually starting to feel less depressed and I am starting to become a good father again. I have read a few spiritual books like The Four Agreements, and A New Earth. I was convinced that spirituality was the answer. But when I read your book it was an instant spiritual awakening, now knowing that I can feel good all the time. I have begun to practice feeling good and guess what? It feels good!

Thank you again for sharing what you have learned. That is very loving of you! I will continue to read your book and continue to practice feeling good and continue to practice love." —A., Ottawa, Ontario

"Something (ego?) is giving way inside me. Feel lighter & happier since reading your book. Peace & Gratitude prevails."
—@HereToBeFree, via Twitter

"Thanks so much for sharing your experience. It was worth it just to be in your presence and energy. I love your idea and I'll start applying it now.

I sometimes experience moments of empowering joy, particularly when in the company of trees or the moon, but also at seemingly inexplicable times, and I always appreciate that feeling…but the concept of consciously working to make that feeling grow is something that hadn't occurred to me until I heard it from you. Thanks for helping me take it to a new level!

Sometimes I experience these moments of joy when walking alone in a crowd of strangers. At these times, I feel I might begin to dance rather than walk, without even knowing it (something your experience in Staples reminded me of).

On my way home from the grocery store tonight, I listened to my mp3 player on the 'shuffle songs' setting, and I came across a song I didn't even know I had. Somehow this song reminded me of you. It just gave me a strong feeling of joy and happiness, and it felt like the same energy I got from you. I've attached it, as I wanted to share it with you. Thanks, and I hope to meet you again."—Faye, Ottawa

"Much joy and much light. Thank you for shining and reflecting so much light in your corner and believing in the ripple effect!"
—@Shekhinahshaman, via Twitter

"I have been practicing joy with Cindy for more than 12 hours over the last four weeks. With the simple, yet very efficient method she proposes, I was able to greatly increase my ability to feel good in all circumstances."—C., Ottawa, Ontario

Based on the simple and powerful practice that is altering lives,
The Alchemy of Love and Joy™

Alchemy
How to Feel Good No Matter What

The treasure is within you…

A true story of human transformation
and a powerful way to shift your state
and turn your world around.

CINDY TEEVENS

Published by Go Beyond
www.alchemylovejoy.com

Teevens, Cindy
Alchemy, How to Feel Good No Matter What / Cindy Teevens

Body - Mind - Spirit
1. Self-help 2. Happiness 3. Spirituality

Cover design: Ronda Taylor, Taylor By Design

PRINTED IN CANADA

Books are available at quantity discounts when used to promote select products or services, or for use in study groups or by associations. For information or to apply, contact the publisher: info@gobeyond.ca

U.S. National Crisis Hot Lines

Suicide Line
1-800-784-2433

Talk Line
1-800-273-8255

Deaf Hotline
1-800-799-4TTY (4889)

or in an emergency dial 911

Canadian National Crisis Hot Lines

Crisis Line
1-866-996-0991

Kids Help Phone
1-800-668-6868

Deaf Hot Line (TDD)
1-800-567-5803

or in an emergency dial 911

There are also specific crisis lines for problems like child or elder abuse, drugs, alcohol, domestic violence, cancer, aids, rape, depression, etc. You can search the internet for a crisis line for your specific needs or call one of the above.

With Gratitude

There is no separation, and we are never alone on a journey. The creation of this book has been touched by innumerable beings. So it belongs to all, and the practice of *The Alchemy of Love and Joy*™ is available free to all through the website.

The paths of other people like my Father Ray (who has changed his perspective, not his location), Eckhart Tolle, Byron Katie, Esther and Jerry Hicks, Jacques, Chris, Lynn, Margarita Khen Nguyen (who spoke no English but embodied the universal language of love and joy), and Dan Millman (*Way of the Peaceful Warrior*) have all led me through mine.

Love and gratitude also go to my other teachers along the way, some now helping from a "higher" perspective: Uncle Tom, John Sweetnam, my Great Uncle Percy, Bruna, Mom, cousin Steve, Reta, Frances Paquette, Dad Larry, Georgette, and Dana.

The Alchemy of Love and Joy™ won the "Next Top Spiritual Author" contest in 2010. Upon receiving the contract I was not moved to sign it. With many publishing options available, it took weeks of research and consideration before the decision became known to me, and I am very thankful for the input of Dan Millman (*Way of the Peaceful Warrior*), Dave Chilton (*The Wealthy Barber*), Steve Weber (*Plug Your Book*), Brad Bunnin (publishing lawyer and author: *The Writer's Legal Companion*), Richard Curtis (*How to Be Your Own Literary Agent*), and Sherna Khambatta (literary agent).

Book publishing is much like horse racing; although you prepare and work hard, the final outcome is dependent upon countless variables: the competition, the riders, the surface, the weather, and providence. Of course, since it is much like gambling on a horse, none of these people knew for sure which was the best way to go, and I am very grateful to them all for contributing their expert offerings and opinions.

It was a magical moment when the *Alchemy* questions found their way from me to Dana, where they worked for her and brought the realization that I must write and share this.

The world has moved to make this message known, and I am amazed and thankful for investment and encouragement from Teong Tan Hin (formerly a "stranger" half-way around the world in Singapore!); the offerings of videographer Richard Lalancette; the technical wizardry as well as the support and encouragement from Gleb Esman, and editorial assistance from Nedra Nash during the first draft, and Stephanie Gunning during the contest.

Thank you to Joanne Sprott for your editing insight, attention to detail, professionalism, and humor, and to Kai Madrone for the divine timing, clarity contribution, and polish in editing the final advance copies.

Support is flowing in from all over the globe, as are the personal accounts of people altering their lives through applying *The Alchemy of Love and Joy*™. You are all critical to making this message known, and I am so grateful for your generosity!

And, I am utterly, unspeakably thankful for the gift of infinite love that led to joy.

Cindy

al-che-my

1: seemingly magical power or process of transmuting

2: an ancient practice focused on changing base metals into gold

3: an analogy for human transformation

Dedication

To Raymond Teevens,
devoted father who raised me with love,
and gave all he could.

Promise fulfilled, with infinite love.

~

And in memory of Larry Wilcox,
the father who I came to know, love, and
cherish as an adult.

Their roles in my life taught me
we can love more than one,
that there is no ration, no limit on love;
and the more you give, the more you get.

Contents

TURNING LEAD INTO GOLD

REAL LIFE EXAMPLES

BEYOND BELIEF

PRACTICE SHEET

EPILOGUE

Speaking the Unspeakable

The explosion of love was followed by a dropping away of space and time, of self and other, of subject and object, and an irrefutable, conclusive direct seeing of myself as *the trees—followed by a cellular tickling that triggered uncontrollable laughter from head to toe, infusing me with the most amazing joy and gratitude until the sun went down.*

The moment that I fell to my knees in the woods crying with the intensity of a massive explosion of love is not one that I thought I could ever explain or share.

I still don't.

Yet a few months before, when considering the realizations that were coming to me, the thought "I can't share that" was immediately countered by "Don't hold back." Indeed, I have not held back since being gifted with joy and compelled to write the book. So I will not hold back now, either.

After the laughter in the woods, however, I went silent, inside and out for a month, unable to even contemplate what to do with something I had never experienced before, and had no reference point from which to understand it myself, never mind from which to share it.

It is ineffable. Unspeakable.

That first seeing happened about nine months after discovering joy, and I almost threw this book out because it seemed to make everything redundant. Yet I recognize that there may be value here for people; after all, *Alchemy* changed my experience of this existence from one of suffering to peace, love, and joy. Yet more importantly, the resultant clearing away of belief in and *as* thought (which you will come to understand as you read this book), seems necessary for direct seeing.

When I work with people who are hurting and witness the "ah-ha's" and the transformations, I can't not act. So, as long as there are people hurting who seek help, I will stand in the shadow of the valley of death with them, and hold the door open.

I will also try to speak the unspeakable and share that experience in the woods to those interested, including what I had been discovering just days prior, what was happening the moment before everything changed, and my processing and integration of it later. For now many of these intimate sharings will be divulged primarily to my friends and close, regular subscribing readers on the website.

If nothing else, there is value, hope, and faith in just knowing that there *is* something else, something beyond what was previously known or could be imagined, something else so unspeakably unknowable as thought, yet intensely real and utterly peaceful, loving, and joyful going on here. Have great faith in that, and great doubt in everything else you thought you knew, because what you thought you knew is what has kept you from it.

I look forward to open, intimate sharing with you, and all your input. You are invited to leave questions or comments on any page of my site: http://www.AlchemyLoveJoy.com

I will read all and reply to as many as I can.
Peace and joy,
Cindy

CHAPTER 1

We Don't Want Things, People, or Events. We Want the Feeling We Mistake Them For.

Eleven-serving-eight!
Waaatook!

A woman smashed the birdie as I reached for my water bottle.

"What did you think of the movie the other night?" Julie asked me.

"It was okay," I said.

"It was depressing, wasn't it?" she said sadly, looking to me for confirmation.

"Things don't depress me," I replied, as I stretched my shoulders.

"Huh?" Her head turned towards me, voice and eyebrows raised in unison.

"Things don't depress me, events don't stress me, and people don't hurt me, no matter what. Well, not since 2009."

"Really? What happened?"

"Well, I went through about six weeks of intense suffering: emotional, psychological, and mental suffering. At its peak, it stopped and then all that energy flipped over into the most amazing joy, peace, love…and even bliss."

Now Julie was fully engaged, and curiosity piqued, her whole body turned towards me as she moved in closer.

"I learned that we don't want things, people, or events. We want the feeling we mistake them for," I continued. Pausing for a moment, she considered that, and slowly nodded because something in it rang true for her, and I could almost see the thoughts and questions swirling.

"Let me ask you this, have you ever felt good on a sunny day?"

"Yes."

"Have you ever felt good on a rainy day?"

"Yes."

"Have you ever felt bad on a sunny day?"

"Yes."

"So it's not about the weather, is it?"

"Ha—no," she laughed.

"Have you ever seen a couple kiss and you felt good?"

"Yes."

"Have you ever seen a couple kiss and you felt bad?"

"Hmm....Yes."

"So it's not about what's happening *outside* you, is it?"

"Uh, no," came the blank admission.

"So what is it about?"

"Me. How I feel."

"That's right; your state."

Yesssss! Twelve-serving-eight.

"If you don't feel bad, there is no problem, no matter what is going on outside you—rain or shine. For example, can you think about a specific time when you had a problem? Got one?" Julie nods.

"Okay, now, if you did not feel bad, would there be a problem?" She paused to consider that, checked within, and admitted, "No, I guess not."

"There might be things to do, right? You might still have things you want to do, but there is no problem, right?"

"Rigghht," she slowly but firmly agreed, as realization set in.

"You'd just do those things feeling good, wouldn't you?"

"Yes, I guess so."

"We've been thinking our problems were outside things, but what we really want is a feeling," I continued, "—and you can give it to yourself any time."

Woooohooo! Thirteen-serving-eight.

"Huh?" up went her eyebrows again. "But how?"

"Well it's got to do with your most powerful and intimate tools: awareness, attention, and interest. Like for example—are you feeling your left foot right now?" Suddenly, she shifted her weight from her left foot to her right and looked at me in surprise.

"No…well, I guess I am now—now that you mentioned it. You also made me realize that I had been standing on one foot for some time and it needed a rest."

"So what happened—had your foot stopped feeling?"

"Well, no" she chuckled. "I just wasn't paying attention to it."

"Right. That was a contraction of attention, away from the whole of your experience onto just what I was saying, essentially eliminating your foot, in your experience, *even though it needed a rest.* Then you became interested in your foot, and that was followed by a very fast shift of attention onto it."

Gotchaa! Fourteen-serving-eight. Game-bird!

"Okay, now, can you feel the top of your head?"

"Yes."

"Can you feel your right shoulder?"

"Yes."

"Did you notice the movement of attention, the shift?"

"Yes!"

"That's your power of attention and ability to move it. Okay, now—what happened to your foot?"

"Hahaha! I forgot about it."

"Notice that you can be aware of your foot and your head and your shoulder at the same time."

"Huh. Yes. Okay, and how does this apply to feeling good?"

"Well, as you notice your feet…and the top of your head… and the walls around you…and your breathing…all at the same time…what happens?"

"There's an expansion," she says as she lets out a breath, "and a relaxation."

"Right. Your attention, previously narrowed on thought, expands as you put attention into the senses, in effect taking some attention and power away from the stream of thinking. Already that feels a little better. With most people attention just wanders, but just like breathing, you can take conscious control of it. Okay, now, sitting there, tell me, have you ever felt better?"

"Well—yah!" she laughed.

"Can you do it now?" Immediately, she went inside, checked in, and her body straightened, and a smile began to curl, quickly followed by a slightly surprised look.

"You just felt a little better, didn't you?"

Yahhhhhhhhhhhhhhh! Game over.

"Um…ya, I guess so," she answered, slightly perplexed. "Okay, but I'm just standing here playing badminton. You said no matter what—what about a bad situation?"

"Okay. Let's use a very specific 'bad' situation. Can you think of one?"

"Uhmmm…"

Next! Cindy, Jan, Julie, and Karen!

"Oh, we're on," I said.

"Cindy? Can we talk more about this?" Grabbing my racquet I said, "Sure! Think of a bad situation while on the court," as I turned away.

~

"So, did anything come to you?" I asked.

"No, actually, on the court I was not thinking—hahaha—that's why I play." I nodded as we shared a knowing grin.

"Okay let's use a fairly common situation. Have you ever felt disconnected from someone you loved?"

"Yes."

"What did you want?"

"Well, connection."

"Okay, feeling disconnected, how do you act?"

"Distant. I pull away. Become quiet."

"Right. Okay, and how will that get you the connection you want?"

"Uh…it won't." She answered sheepishly.

"What if you could feel connected *first?* How would you act then? And how much more likely would that be to get connection on the outside?"

"Much more," came her timid reply.

"That's how to be the change you want to see in the world. How valuable is that?"

"Very! How?"

"In order to learn how there are many things you must unlearn. And to simply remember what you have been able to do since birth—feel good."

~

24

That conversation arose spontaneously as a result of no longer being able to support thinking and beliefs that fuel mental and emotional discomfort or suffering. False thoughts like "He hurt me" and "It stresses me" began to jump out and glare at me. They are no longer part of my vocabulary.

Since discovering the power of love and joy, and this ability we all have, my experience of life has transformed no matter what is going on around me. Peace and happiness are my predominant companions, and the frequency and intensity of joyful and plea-surable experiences have multiplied without any outside reason. While it was pain and suffering that prompted me to seek joy, it was not the pain and suffering that gave it to me. It was the joy.

We do not *have* to hurt, but like a child learning to walk who bumps into things, we can use the pain to push off from, and to discover our inherent freedom and joy.

Where my story truly starts or ends I cannot know; however, when I first sat down to write about this discovery, what initially emerged was a painful story from the past. While I personally rarely have use for the past, I present some of it here so that you can relate and know that there is nothing more special about me than you. We all suffer the same, and just the same, we can all know our inherent joy.

This next short chapter covers a painful period of my life, which was a major catalyst in my search for an end to inner suf-fering. It brings into the open one of society's most feared events; an event that we could all agree is a "good reason" to suffer. However, that would only serve to prolong the pain and support beliefs that have sustained suffering, which we are outgrowing. Society must take a leap in consciousness, and it is obviously ready because many people are already leaping.

I have come to know that even a trauma of this scale cannot take away your inherent peace. Even something on this scale does not mean we *must* suffer. There is no darkness deep enough that can exist in the presence of even the smallest light.

Bear with me through this story; like all suffering, this story will end and in the comparative grand scheme of things, it is short. This story comes with gratitude, for without it I may not have sought, found, nor been able to share the love and joy which has no need and no object; the infinite, eternal joy of Being.

CHAPTER 2

There's No Such Thing as a Beginning, and Here We Are.

The last four days have almost been continuously like this. Shivers tingling up and down my body give rise to goose bumps. I beam at strangers everywhere I go—and they beam back!

Even sitting alone, smiling, my happiness and pleasure grow without reason. My thoughts now bring me joy and peace. Just breathing is pleasure. It wasn't always like this, though…

Massive shock and grief overwhelmed me. I curled into a sobbing ball and intense wave after wave of pain and suffering racked my shaking body. A voice not my own welled up and wailed out from some unknown place within me. It was like something out of a movie, unreal, yet actually happening.

I knew something was seriously wrong when my father did not answer the phone all weekend. Family members who tried to call him did not reach him either. Everyone said not to worry, which I think was a healthy response, but my gut was gnawing. Monday was his birthday, and every year I went over to his house with dinner. Still, there was no answer and his voice mail was full. That was it. I could not take it anymore. I raced across the city.

My heart sank as I approached the dark house and noticed that the snow had not been plowed in days. His backyard, vehicles, paths, and steps were always neatly cleared of snow. Never as a child or an adult had I seen this. Even though it was his trade, his truck and plow sat still in his driveway, covered with undisturbed snow. Grabbing the flashlight he gave me for Christmas, I trudged through the snow and into the dark house alone, calling for him. No answer. Was he not home?

Finally brave enough to be quiet and scared enough to be still, I heard his heavy breathing. It was almost his snore, familiar and somewhat relieving. "Dad? Dad!" I called into the dark bedroom. Why was he not answering? I reached for the light switch. Oh my god Dad, *what have you done?!* My poor father, unable to bear his hellish burden anymore, was now barely breathing, his life energy draining.

Stomach-churning anxiety rocketed through me. But there was no time for that; the snoring meant that Dad was still alive, still breathing. I needed to act, so I attempted to clear my mind.

The woman on the 9-1-1 service called the police for me, and then asked me if there was anyone else in the house, further frightening me. Considering the events in Dad's life up to then, including the multiple major depressions he had struggled with, and the undisturbed snow, I dismissed the idea of an intruder. She said the ambulance was on its way, but that the paramedics would not be allowed to enter until the house was empty and secured by police. That meant I had to leave.

Leave Dad?! He could be dying! Torn, at first I said no, I could not do that—but that meant they would not help him, and I was not helping him. Knowing time was of the essence, even as inwardly I yelled "*No!,*" my physical actions complied.

As the approaching sirens screamed through the air and red and blue flashes of police lights lit up the sky, I left Dad. Out in the cold night I slid to the ground against a cruiser's wheel, screaming in anguish and disbelief. An officer offered me a place in the backseat, where a claustrophobic feeling began to grow. Discovering I was locked in, a powerless, claustrophobic feeling further consumed me. I bounced back and forth from side to side, shaking and crying uncontrollably. Finally, after a painfully long time, the ambulance arrived and the police allowed the medics into the house. Time crawled even more slowly.

Just as they were loading Dad into the ambulance, I heard over the radio that my brother had arrived. My family had known I was coming over and when they did not hear from me, my brother decided to follow. From a distance, I could hear and sense his pained reaction to the news. I wanted so badly to go to him, but the police would not let me. In fact, I was told they would not even let me go to the hospital! Instead, I was to be taken to the police station for questioning.

"How much more could a person take?" I wondered. This was a question I would ask myself over and over during the next seven days.

Events continued to seem surreal: being questioned at the station; waiting as Dad went through emergency surgery; getting the news from the doctor that he was now on life support; telling arriving family members what happened and preparing them, as best as they could be prepared mentally and emotionally, for what they would see when they saw him.

I relayed information between the doctors and my family, explaining how within a few days, once the drugs wore off and he came to, whatever degree he would come "to," whatever mental and physical functions he had then, were going to be it…forever. Distinctly, I remember talking on the phone to a family member , describing what had happened, while thinking, "This is so unreal."

After having being interrogated as the potential killer—another unreal experience—and being cleared, mostly due to the suicide note Dad left, which I had not seen, I was offered victim counseling. Oh how things change—and on a dime. First the police counselor, and then the hospital's counselor gave me empathy, support, and suggestions of "walking, talking, and tears." Mostly their encouragement was to talk (and I guess with that to cry) in order to "share" what had happened, which basically meant reliving it repeatedly.

I had recently begun studying Zen, so I asked for, and began receiving assistance and guidance from the monks. At the time, their directions seemed to make no sense, yet these directions enabled me to function and to do what I had to do while minimizing my suffering (and thereby minimizing the suffering of others) as much as possible. The monks recommended *not* talking about the event, *not* reliving it. I agreed, thinking once was enough!

If I had been unable to talk about it, that might have been different. But the tears that came, came not one extra, not one less for choosing not to relive the trauma. It was enough to be in the moment with what was. Other advice I received in the hospital, to walk and to sit in the sun, I did take and found helpful.

But none of that happened until later, because I only left the hospital once in seven days. During that week, Dad's eyes would flutter when he heard people's voices, but that was it. He never spoke, he never consciously moved. The whole family knew he would not like to "live" like this, and so we mutually gave permission to remove him from life support.

The doctors did not know how long he might live without life support; it could be minutes, hours, days, or weeks, but not likely months. Removing life support was a powerful experience, all of us around him, offering love, prayers, thoughts, and energy, while watching the tubes being removed and waiting to see whether or not he'd take a breath on his own. He did. And there it was again, that familiar, deep, peaceful snore.

I listened to that snore day and night in the chair beside the bed until the morning it mixed with the sound of pigeons cooing near the open window, and this new sound woke me just before the phone rang. I leapt up so fast that for a dazed moment I thought I had disturbed Dad. "Odd thought," I thought. Scrambling around the bed to the phone on the other side, I noticed Dad had deteriorated a lot. His breathing was shallow, his skin was grey, and there was a palpable, yet indescribable drop in life energy.

As I chatted with Mom on the phone, I touched Dad's arm. It seemed cooler than usual. Then I noticed that his breathing had slowed to being almost imperceptible, and he was pausing longer before inhaling. Before death, or passing over, breathing often pauses for a moment, then resumes. Closer to the moment of transition, it pauses longer.

Dad had been getting closer and closer every day, so while I was on the phone, I began to time him and realized he was rapidly deteriorating. Mom's voice faded into the background as my attention shifted completely onto him. Watching the clock, I realized this was his moment. "Mom, Mom…" I interrupted whatever it was she was saying, "This is it. He stopped breathing."

She stopped mid-sentence, "Whaaat? Are you sure? Time him," she pleaded.

"I have been timing him since getting on the phone, and he has not taken another breath in over thirty seconds," I said. We had only been on the phone a few minutes when he took his last breath. It was utterly peaceful and perfectly timed. Last call. It seemed as though he waited for Mom, with whom he shared a strong mutual love, despite living apart from her, to connect with him somehow before he transitioned.

Looking back, "transition" is the ideal word. At the time, it was strange to experience "death" as a gradual thing, because in my mind death was an ending. Endings are normally clearly defined, even abrupt. But this was almost a non-event. I began to wonder what exactly death is. Was it lack of breathing? Was it lack of a heartbeat? Was it lack of brain activity? Obviously there was some brain activity going on, but could that be called "life?" It would seem through this experience that death is when there is no more inhalation after a certain length of time, but somehow I knew that was not it either. I knew what death *wasn't*, yet I could not tell what it *was*.

I lost track of where life starts and ends. Later, I came to know that there is no beginning, and no end. That birth and death, that arising, dwelling, and decaying—that *change*—is what life does, and that change is not an end. It is change. The limited, linear mind thinks in sentences, in parts, in separation; it draws lines where there are none. These lines become beliefs, such as a belief in death as an end and even a belief in birth as a beginning. We mentally take these divisions to be true, and so the flow of experience, which is undivided, inevitably clashes with the mind.

At the time, there was not much opportunity to contemplate these things. Mom was stunned for a moment, and then the pain of loss and the mourning began. There were many living, breathing people to attend to and to notify. There was still much going on, many things to take care of, and more people on the way.

People came from long distances, bringing with them their experiences and memories of Dad. Pieces of his life offered by different relatives who knew different events that had led up to the this trauma came together. In an attempt to comprehend, the usual habit is to ask why and to look for a reason, as if a reason would ease the pain.

But no one thing was "responsible," nothing stood out separately from the rest. There were so many things; the stroke his best friend and boarder had suffered in Dad's truck and Dad holding faith that he would recover, keeping his room available for him; the government taking over the boarder's affairs and delaying the release of rent money owed to Dad; his difficulty finding work; his inability to keep up with his expenses; threats from the hydroelectric company to shut off the power; borrowing money and getting deeper into financial trouble; his drinking and apparent attempt to stop drinking (there was no alcohol in his blood, nor any bottles in his home when he died); his multiple severe depressions; the drugs he was on; and on and on. Certainly I could not blame Dad, he suffered so much. I saw each event metaphorically, as a "nail" in his coffin.

As the clues and stories emerged about why he would have attempted to die by suicide, a bigger picture became quite clear to me: *there is no such thing as a separate life.* Everything and everyone who touched Dad's life *made* his life. Everything and everyone has a seamlessly intermeshed place, and we can never know how one little action, or inaction, affects another's life. You will never know the bigger picture effects you have on others—you never know how far a change will go.

{ Pain is not personal; it belongs to every human being alive.
~ Debbie Ford }

When I sat down to write, I did not know that Dad's story would come out. I did not know the powerful impact it would have on so many other people's lives. It has become apparent to me, however, that there is no beginning and there is no end. You are another example. This happened, I wrote, and you are reading. Everything we do and don't do affects another and, in that way, affects everyone.

That is how important you are.

Yet, even while knowing we are not separate, there can be a sense of separation. Dazed after Dad transitioned, I slowly walked out of the hospital and realized that nobody I passed in the hallway knew what had just happened. I was surrounded by people, but I felt completely alone; it all seemed surreal again. As I made my way through the hospital lobby, contemplating this along with Dad's and everyone else's suffering, I made a promise to him that "it would not be for nothing." Then I stopped at a kiosk where I bought a ring as a reminder of my intent. I had no clue what "not for nothing" meant, but I vowed that I would find out.

What I would later discover was far beyond anything I could have ever imagined.

CHAPTER 3

My Quest

It took about three months to recover to the point where this trauma was not an everyday suffering for me. There was grief, sorrow, and sadness, but not a whole lot of added mental wrestling or suffering, or it would have lasted longer I'm sure. Still, the experience was one of the greatest, longest, and most intense sufferings in my life—and it was one of the greatest gifts I've ever received as it unwittingly started me on a quest to find an end to suffering.

There have been sufferings since, yet most seemed to pale in comparison; and as I compared them an awareness *of* the suffering began to arise. I began to see the suffering and not so much lose myself in it—to less and less become it. Here I am, the watcher, seeing suffering and *there* it is, the suffering. It and I are not one and the same. When we "become" the suffering it seems as if there *is* nothing else. It seems there is no option, no choice but to "go through it," as if there is some dictated length of time that needs to pass, or some unknown things that need to happen for it to end. When we wake up from suffering and to the rest of the world (which is always already there), suffering stops, seemingly magically, on its own.

Having become aware of suffering, a new form of suffering arose in me…the *seeing* of my suffering, not wanting it, and simultaneously *not being able to change it*. At least, that was my belief at the time.

The Dalai Lama says that pain is inevitable, and that suffering is optional. Nice thought, I thought, but how does one *live* it? Simply thinking the thought, "I don't want to suffer," does not change the experience. In fact, it puts your attention and focus on the pain and causes more. Trying to deny, hide, or push suffering away does not work for the same reason. Accepting suffering, as in believing it to be necessary and all there is, also does not change the suffering and sometimes intensifies it.

Nothing seemed to help, and just months before this tragic event, I already felt like no one understood me or related to me. I felt lonely and began to wonder if religion held the answer and for a while became intensely driven to find meaning in life, or a religion I could resonate with, or even just people who thought like I did. It was all in vain. I felt utterly alone and like everything was pointless.

Then I came across the little book, *Buddhism, Plain and Simple* by Steve Hagen. From this book I somehow came to understand that there wasn't even a "me" here *to* feel alone. That news sent me spiraling into three days of painful suffering, feeling like I had died. (Obviously, I also had a belief that death is suffering.)

At the end of the three days, lying on the floor with the suffering just beginning to ease, I noticed and heard the thought "but my heart is still beating."

"I," or who I thought "I" was, was dead—but I was still alive! For a moment, I believe my mind stopped. I stood up and almost immediately switched from suffering to joy. Laughter burst out as I saw the absurdity of who I had thought myself to be, now gone. For three days I laughed and lived in bliss.

A big part of me, the "me" I believed in, the idea of a separate me—separated from all else—(which I did not know *was* the cause of suffering), had largely died. I say "largely" because it was not quite complete and over time, the bliss and clarity leveled out. I came back "down." I did not know what exactly had happened or how to "sustain" it. However, I never quite went back to where I had been, either. After glimpsing the truth about suffering and the truth of what is, there is no going back.

For two years after Dad's passing life became quiet and mostly peaceful. At some point, life seemed to become almost boring; I was not learning anything. There was some inner drive building; was it the impulse of life to grow, to expand, to become more? Perhaps it was a sense that something was not complete. Something was missing.

A desire to be challenged and to grow through relationship arose in me. I actually remember making a conscious decision that that was what I wanted. I wanted to learn and transform, but had no real awareness of into what, or how. I remember verbalizing the word "challenge" to friends. Our intentions appear to hold immense power, so I was to learn.

CHAPTER 4

My Path

With a self, otherwise known as "ego" intact, relationships are certainly a way to be challenged. Usually without the same intensity of pain and blindness that violent trauma can trigger, relationships can clearly mirror and give space and opportunity to see what is inside you, if you have the intention and the courage to look there.

Going inside, I began to question all my experiences, my thoughts, and my perceptions about others. I did this alone or with a close friend who knew my intention and who was willing to explore various perspectives and possibilities beyond my usual thoughts. Then, through Byron Katie's book *Loving What Is*, I discovered I was *not* my thoughts, and later it became obvious that they were not even "my" thoughts. After all, if they were, then I could just turn them off, right?

THOUGHTS COME AND GO, AND BELONG TO NOBODY

Ever notice that everyone has pretty much the same thoughts like "I am not good enough" or "It should not have happened"? So how is it that we claim ownership? Also, You can't hold a thought longer than seconds, and then it has to be, well, re-thought. Thoughts do not stay—it is impossible to grasp or "claim" them. Thoughts can actually be measured outside the brain. They arise without warning, and they come and go, and belong to nobody.

We are like radios, we can "pick them up," know, and experience thoughts. But we don't *have* to. We can't control them, but we can flip through the frequencies, skip them, stop wherever we want, and leave them whenever we want. If we have not practiced that awareness and ability though, then like broken records, we can get stuck on a frequency, replaying painful thoughts over and over, believing a single particular thought, mistaking it for truth beyond all other thoughts and possibilities, as if it were the most important thing, or even as if there is nothing else. When *that* happens, we can even believe ourselves to *be* our thoughts.

The evidence of this is built into our language. Take for example the sentence "I am angry." Of course *you* are not anger. *You* are not your thoughts. How can you be that which you are aware of? You know, experience, and are aware of your hand, but you are not your hand. You can experience and know anger. And you can lose who you really are in the belief that you *are* anger and that you have no other choice but to feel and act like anger. You can even use it as a rationalization or an excuse: "Well, I was angry!"

Thoughts are just a tiny part of our experience and capability. You are a much larger being that can open to intelligence far beyond a tiny, fleeting, unsubstantial thought.

Thoughts don't do anything

As you sit, lie, or stand there reading, you are seeing, right? Do your eyes tell you that you are seeing? Do you need the thought "I am seeing" in order to see? You are also hearing, right? Do your ears tell you that you are hearing? Do you need a thought to tell you that? Do you need a thought in order to hear?

As you hold this book and read, just for a moment, drop all of the painful beliefs, thoughts, and ideas that have repeated and plagued your mind. Ready? Okay, go!

~

You may notice…you are still breathing, right? You don't really need those thoughts, do you?

When you put one foot in front of the other and walk, do you need to think about it? When you are washing the dishes, do you need to think "Go around, and around, and around, and around…"? As far as your being, your presence, your experience, your life, you do not need thoughts for *anything*.

> { *The Centipede's Dilemma*
> A centipede was happy quite,
> Until a frog in fun
> Said, "Pray, which leg comes after which?"
> This raised her mind to such a pitch,
> She lay distracted in the ditch
> Considering how to run.
> ~ Mrs. Edmund Craster }

You are not your thoughts. *You are before thought*; that is how you can know thought. Yes, thoughts, which are closely tied to speech have practical value—like differentiating when you wish to communicate with Luke and not Mary—but apart from that, they actually don't *do* anything and they are not critical to your being.

Not only do thoughts not do anything, they also can't *stop* you from doing anything. If you have ever done something like running for exercise, you know you could be putting on your running shoes or stepping out the door even as you think "I don't feel like it." *But it's just a thought*. You can notice thoughts, and keep doing.

Parents, students, children, athletes, employees, homemakers—everyone—has had many experiences of "not wanting to do" something, but of doing it anyway. Often, once you are doing, you find it is not so bad and you may even begin enjoying what you are doing. It never was or is the doing that feels bad, it is the believed bad thought about doing *itself*.

Thoughts are not intelligence

{ Mind is just a reflex organ. Reacts to everything.
Fills your head with millions of random thoughts a day.
~ Socrates character (Nick Nolte) in the movie, *Peaceful Warrior* }

I was chatting with a friend who told me a story about seeing an airplane cross the sky as she sat in a restaurant when the thought, "What would I do if that airplane blew up right now?" came to her awareness.

How many bizarre thoughts have you "had," or more accurately, noticed—and tossed? Why did you not claim them as "yours" and take them as seriously as you might other thoughts, designed to make you suffer? You *know* that some thoughts are pointless, and that you do not have to believe or act on every one that you notice. If you don't act on every one, then you don't *have* to act on every (or any) thought, even if a feeling arises at the same time. The difference is whether you have interest in it or not.

Thoughts can trigger feelings (and vice versa). If the thought is believed, and it is a negative thought, so will the feeling be. Just because you feel the effect of a negative thought does not mean the thought is true; *it means you are experiencing a negative feeling thought.*

To know for sure if the thought behind the feeling is true or not, you need to see with clear vision—you need to see, hear, know, and think *without* the bad feeling. Bad feeling states can become quite thick and convincing, regardless of whether the accompanying believed thoughts are true or not.

Clearing the feeling will not make you "vulnerable," and it will not make you make the wrong choice. No matter how you are feeling, good or bad, you still have choice. The question is: Is your choice based upon clear seeing and intelligence? Or is it blindly driven by a bad feeling?

Suffering is a focusing-in on one thing to the exclusion of everything else; it is a contraction. Focused attention is linear and can narrow onto one object at a time, appearing to slice and dice reality into moments and components. The result: a lack of information, and you are left with a tiny piece of the whole picture in your experience. Until the (believed) bad feeling is cleared, you may seem to have fewer options and little or no apparent choice.

When you're suffering all you see is what you don't want. That *is* what suffering *is*. When you have a bad feeling, all manner of bad ideas will flow to you to "support" it. They can convince you that the bad feeling is real and justified, and your imagination can run wild with false thoughts stacked upon one another.

{ You can't depend on your eyes when your imagination
is out of focus. ~ Mark Twain }

Suffering is a contraction, a movement away from your inherent love, joy, and freedom, and relief is an expansion. Clearing the feeling will open you to more of what is actually going on, allow access to infinite intelligence, give you more options, and enable you to make the most ecological choices and take the most beneficial actions. Ecological choices take into account everything and everyone around you; they are (w)holistic in value and completeness. Acting on a narrow, bad feeling limits you, makes you vulnerable to ignorance, can cause additional suffering in yourself, and can trigger it in others. Choosing love over pain or fear feels good.

{ Go to the truth beyond the mind. Love is the bridge.
~ Stephen Levine }

THOUGHTS ARE NOT INHERENTLY TRUE

Thoughts just are. As a single, tiny, narrow attempt to explain a vast experience, they must, by nature, exclude much of reality—a very large portion, actually! Words come out in a string, singularly, one after another, yet the whole of reality is seamless, simultaneous and multiplistic. So much information is lost with thought. If a thought represented one degree of the 360 degrees of reality (and that would be being generous), and, if you believe it without a doubt to be your absolute, whole reality and truth, then you are 359 degrees blind.

If you are relying on a thought to dictate how you feel and what you can experience, then you are also 100% out of control of your life because you can't control thoughts any more than you can control the weather.

When you believe a thought while feeling bad, then that thought is not based on reality "out there," it is based on your fears and needs inside; so it is not in alignment with reality or truth "out there." You will be prone to misinterpreting events and people negatively, causing suffering for yourself and others. To be in alignment with love and truth, or reality, clear seeing must be internal before it can be external.

Wisdom comes from clarity, from a vast intelligence that includes and embraces the whole situation, all the factors, and all the other people involved; both the context and ecology.

Let's look closely at a typical painful thought: "He is needy." Packs an emotional punch, right? If we tried to include more reality (truth) by adding context and ecology to that statement, it could become: "He is needy, when I want to do something else" or "…when his child is sick" or "…when he's fixing our bathroom." The more ecology and context you bring in, the closer you come to truth, and the better it feels. What about "He is needy by asking for help…when I have better things to do than give time, understanding, acceptance, or love."

The better you feel, the more context and ecology (access to wisdom, compassion, and love) you have. "Oh, okay, there are times when he's not needy, and there are times when I need him." What just happened to the feeling? Is that possibly also true, or even more true? What happened to the original belief? Which experience do you prefer?

A single thought, removed from the wisdom of context and ecology (the totality of reality), *cannot* represent truth. Inevitably, if believed and acted upon as such, it will cause suffering.

Given all this, we can even say that *thoughts are inherently* not *true*.

THOUGHTS HAVE NO POWER

Thoughts are like the moon. The moon has no light of its own; it borrows and reflects the light of the sun. Without the light of the sun, the moon is not seen. Without your power, thoughts can harmlessly come and go. Only with the power of your interest, belief, and attention can thoughts come to life in your experience. Otherwise, like the moon, they are essentially invisible and powerless.

You are the power.

Consider the importance of that, because an otherwise harmless thought, with the power of belief, can start a war. The implication is massive; without inner peace there can be no outer peace.

~

CONCEPTUAL THOUGHTS, BELIEVED AS TRUTH,
CAN BE DANGEROUS

You don't need a thought to know a stove is hot. Yet this knowing can be expressed as a practical, factual thought. I can tell you the stove is hot. But you would simply not believe it, nor would *you* say it, if the stove was *not* hot.

On the other hand, a conceptual thought is dangerous because it can be absolutely *anything*. It needs no practical, actual, direct reality as its basis. It can be so *easily* said. It can also be *completely* imaginary. That's okay, because as the nothing that all thoughts are, they will come and go—unless they are believed in, and in essence, brought to life. If they feel bad, then there is a sense of a problem. The other danger of concepts is that because they are not direct truth, they can beg other questions. Because there is no actuality to the original thought, these other questions must be answered with more concepts, and the whole thing can grow into a big, unreal dream—perhaps even a nightmare.

Concepts in and of themselves are not bad, and indeed some are useful for a while, and as long as they are recognized as concepts and not mistaken for truth or reality.

When unquestioned concepts become beliefs, people can cling to their concepts passionately because without them they think that they "know" nothing. (In truth, they already know nothing, except their concept.) Or it can escalate; if they identify with their concepts, then the end of a concept can even be perceived as the end of *themselves*, so people may defend conceptual beliefs violently, feeling it is a matter of life or death.

If you let your conceptual thoughts about your self dissolve, it may even feel like you are dying, as happened to me after three days of suffering, but you will discover that your heart will still be beating. The only thing that can die is what you are *not—a* false concept of who you are.

{ …it is in dying that we are born to eternal life.

~ St. Francis of Assisi }

There are precious few thoughts we share that are not conceptual; most people are living out of conceptual dreams. If all excess concepts and thoughts could not be spoken, people would be saying much less. And there'd be a lot more peace.

We have taught each other numberless concepts such as "part of me is"…"part of me wants"…"part of me won't," and "my higher self," parroting what others before us have said. We have repeated these empty, unsubstantiated conceptual thoughts without *direct* knowing *as* the knowledge. Yet that is what we call knowledge.

You are not a thought

When the Greek sages said *Know thyself*, they did not mean as a thought. They did not mean anything like "I am a Mother, a lawyer, or a coach." They did not mean "I am a strong person, a sensitive person, or a healer." These mere fleeting roles, feelings, limitations, moments, or ideas are not worth the effort or value of carving *Know thyself* in stone.

They are also just single thoughts. Take any one of these thoughts and answer "Is that ALL that I am?" and you will know it is not what you are.

You can say a whole bunch of things about yourself, and still that collection of thoughts is not who or what you are. Even your personality, which was learned, acquired, and conditioned, is constantly changing. It is a collection of thoughts *about* you—and not who you are. In saying *Know thyself*, the Greek sages did not mean to know a *thought* about yourself. They point to a possibility much more vast and far more intimate.

As an analogy for this, you can study honey all your life, you can analyze it and test it all your life, and even write books about honey and become an expert—but until you *taste* honey, you do not *know* honey. Instead of an idea or a conceptual thought about yourself, the Greek sages are pointing to the ultimate, absolute reality and truth of who or what you are.

So when people say conceptual things like: "A part of me just can't let go," I do not let that go. I head-on address the limiting concept. This may appear to be "mere semantics," or just "expressions" as some people object, but if you are brutally honest about it, you will see that *your behavior* is being generated accordingly and is being validated, excused, allowed, or blamed on something supposedly apart from you.

Yet this something, this "part" has no direct reality. Literally —show me it, show me this part. If it speaks with such authority, such power, as if it were truth, then let it step forward and take a stand as to its own true existence. Nothing will come forward, because nothing is there. This "part" is not even separate from you, so how can it be a part? It *is* you—believing in a thought, giving a concept life in your "reality" or more accurately, in your experience.

If this "part" is ultimate truth—if there truly is a "part of you" that won't let go and which you can't do anything about— then why even bother, why not just stop right there and give up?

Closely examined, concepts fall apart and are easily exposed. What you say is important because you say what you believe, and you believe what you say.

If you won't be truthfully clear and honest with yourself about limiting concepts, then you will not know truth and freedom. If it's not grounded in the truth of direct knowing, (and especially if it is not beneficial), then stop saying it. Raise the bar of language. More and more speak only truth, so you will think only truth, and live only truth.

You may need to know that the stove is hot; but you do *not* need to imagine that there are "parts" of you and that they are out of your control. Beware of what otherwise powerless thoughts you give life to in your experience.

{ Throw out the trash. ~ Socrates character in the book,
The Way of the Peaceful Warrior }

Here are some more common limiting concepts I have heard (some I once parroted myself). Unquestioned, they may be believed simply because they arise and are noticed, but *they themselves*, believed in, are the cause of stress:

- He or she stresses me.
- Things around me cause me stress.
- I am just a sensitive person.
- There must be something wrong with me.
- Because of that trauma, I'll never recover.
- Work stresses me.
- That's just the way I am.
- I've never been good enough.
- I have to think more positively.
- Thoughts keep beating me down.

Later on we will prove that you cannot possibly be any of these thoughts (or any others).

TIME TO DROP TIME

{ The past has no power over the present moment.
~ Eckhart Tolle, *The Power of Now* }

Another feature of limiting, suffering thoughts is that they often have time built into them. Look at the previous list, and you'll notice every thought incorporates time (past or future) or memory (past). Even the statement "That's just the way I am" is based on how you were, in the past, and it projects how you will be in the future.

You are holding this book, so if right now you say, "people stress me," you are talking about what has happened in the past and the non-existent future, and your anticipation for it—but right now, as you read, is that true? Is it actually happening…now?

Although time could be used to identify some limits, the best and simplest indicator is how you feel. Anything believed in time is limiting and feels bad.

Even time itself does not exist—it is a concept. When you remember something that happened in the past, you are accessing images, sounds, thoughts, and feelings in the brain *now*.

{ Time perception, just like vision, is a construction of the brain
and is shockingly easy to manipulate experimentally.
~ Brian M. Eagleman, Neuroscience Ph.D., *Brain Time* }

Time is a way to measure *change*. Time was created based on the *changes* of the sun and stars. One example of the need for a way to measure change was so that trains and people could come to the same place together. Without a way to measure the days and hours (Earth's spin), the seasons (Earth's tilt) and the years (Earth's revolutions around the sun) and without a way to share that information, people would never meet trains.

In actual truth, there is only this one field of now where everything changes. There *is* no time. There is only now. Change happens in the now, and the now is spacious and unlimited. It is said that the only constant is change; however, there must also be That Within Which change happens—That which does not change—That which *knows* change.

~

As I speak about the past, I will speak of my experience as it was in the moment, and that will sometimes come in the form of concepts that I believed at the time (and no longer believe or sustain). I include them here so that you may relate, and know that I relate. See if you can notice them as you read; I will subtly mark them, when first used, with a raised asterisk like this: *

Separating the wheat from the chaff, concept from truth, is important. Some concepts can be used as tools, but do not cling to them as truth because then you will be in your own way. Use them, but don't be used by them. Similarly, discretion is also important when it comes to understanding the relationships between thoughts and feelings, and reality.

THINKING IS FAST, FEELING IS SLOW

Because it is the body that feels and because the body is denser than thoughts, which are more subtle, feeling is usually slower to be known than thoughts. Feeling can be slower to build and can also be slower to be recognized because the average person is so involved with thinking that they are not aware of feeling.

Thoughts are so fast that many can whip by before you begin to notice them. But with one strong thought-feeling association, or enough negative thoughts in succession, a bad-feeling state can become predominant and strong enough to catch your attention, and possibly your belief. Unless you begin to reach for a better feeling, unless you begin to awaken joy and intelligence, then that bad-feeling state can trigger more bad thoughts, followed by more bad feelings—and the downward cycle begins.

Once settled into the body, a state can become strong and dense—and density is one piece of "evidence" we use to accept something as real and true. The experience of density has been used to support our beliefs about what is going on; one bad feeling, and we may think the accompanying thought is real or true.

Then *all* of our attention goes into solving this problem-thought, through thinking. This is how we can get deeply lost in a stream of thinking, how we can become unconscious to the totality of reality, and lost to the rest of possible experience and knowing. It is how we can believe false thoughts to be true, to be real.

{ Problems cannot be solved by the same level of thinking that created them. ~ Albert Einstein }

There's an unspoken, false, mass belief that if you hurt *so* much, or feel *so* intensely bad, then what you blame it on must be real. But no matter how badly you feel, you can't hurt enough to make something that is false, true. Certainly, the pain is your experience, but that does not mean the thoughts involved are true.

Everything that has been said about thought can be said about feeling: it is not permanent, it comes and goes, it doesn't *do* anything, it is not intelligence, it is not inherently true, and it has no power (except the power you give it). You can't control feeling (but you don't have to give it the power of your attention), and finally, you are not your feeling. How you feel is something you can *know*—and again, how can you *be* that which you can *know?*

For our purpose, whether or not a thought came first or a feeling came first does not matter. That would be the slippery mind trying to find a "reason" or "outside cause" for a bad feeling to support the bad feeling, to make it "real." *The only thing that matters is awareness of how you feel, good or bad,* because that can be used. So I am now combining the two and calling them "thought-feelings."

After getting lost in negative thought-feeling for some time, you may notice your previously cramped-up body suddenly "drop" and release when stressful thinking stops. In that moment, you have "woken up" out of the stream of negative thinking. In that moment, *you have an opportunity to know something different.* You have an opportunity to use *Alchemy,* and soon I will share how.

MIND-READS

Since current experts believe that lightning-fast thoughts cause and precede feelings (and can even dominate feeling), I, like everyone else, did not question the experts. Yet unquestioned thoughts that become mass beliefs are what can make us sheep, following the herd without a mind of our own, and this is how history repeats itself. When I set off to research thoughts (before I knew them as thought-feelings), I began by questioning everything.

Along the way, I discovered Neuro-Linguistic Programming (NLP), the science, art, and skill of human communication, behavior, and change. Thinking it was "the answer," I trained to the Master Practitioner level and learned much about thoughts. I began to watch thoughts closely, particularly the type of thought that in NLP we call a "mind-read," which is claiming to know someone else's intention or state of being.

The average person mind-reads constantly. For a week I closely watched my tendency to mind-read and discovered, to my horror, not only how often it is done (ad nauseam!), but that almost all of the mind-reads were negative ones that caused suffering, like "He looked at me ugly," "She cut me off," "He did not say hi, he does not like me."

Notice the one common denominator? People or situations are different, but there's *always* a "Me, Me, Me." Mind-reads are *your* thoughts, not someone else's! How insane is it to believe they belong to someone else? They come from and are about you, and their source is *your* fears and hopes, *your* attachments. No wonder acting on mind-reads inherently triggers suffering in ourselves and in others!

I began using a powerful question to discover whether my mind-reads were true for the person on whom I imposed them. I simply asked, "What was the purpose (of saying or doing that)?"

In almost all cases, my mind-read was wrong. How humbling was that! Many of the answers were ones that I could not relate to or could have never thought. My mind stretched with the endless expanse of possible meanings and purposes out there, far beyond my own.

Then it occurred to me, if we are going to mind-read, why not mind-read something nice? So for a couple days, I went around thinking everyone was absolutely magnificent. I made up wonderful mind-reads for everything I saw. Then I realized that I was having a grand time, and so was everyone else! So it became a new habit. When I noticed a bad-feeling mind-read, I reached for a good-feeling one ("true" or not, because how do I know for certain anyway?); and there was balance. Taking it a little further, I created wild, funny mind-reads. What fun! It really devalued my faith in and grip on mind-reads. I stopped taking them so seriously (after all, it *is* only a thought).

Soon I largely quit mind-reading all together. Now, if I really feel driven to know, I get curious and ask the other person, "What was your purpose or intention?" (Never ask, "Why?" That word communicates judgment and causes people to shut down).

The neat thing about this question is that if someone's intent *was* to be hurtful, it brings it to their awareness. It's like a reflex; we automatically answer all questions, at least inside. While you may not get a verbal answer on the outside, the problem tends to disappear because the question makes people accountable to themselves—and we know best, don't we, when we are out of line? We do listen to ourselves much more than to others. This works wonders with perceived sarcasm.

But most importantly, the answers served to shine truth and light on my mind-reads, exposing them for what they were: painful, sometimes petty, and always egoic. It is a humbling, enlightening exercise I encourage everyone to experience.

All this learning about thoughts (which at the time I still thought "caused" pain) was interesting and somewhat useful, but it still was not a reliable end to my internal suffering, nor an end to pain that I could trigger in others, outside.

And it was not always self-defending action that caused pain. How many times, even though your intentions were good, did your actions (or non-actions) backfire and not produce the intended results in others? This utterly baffled me many times.

Your actions may fail to get your intended results because (1) *your* intentions for others are not *theirs*—and do not match theirs, or (2) you form an intention based on a mind-read that is not true for the other.

IT IS THE REASON WE GIVE FOR SUFFERING THAT CREATES IT

When we suffer, we are never hurting because of what someone else did or said. We hurt as a direct result of the thought we have, hold, and believe *about* what they said. (I am not talking about someone physically hurting you; what is being addressed here is mental and emotional pain. You can also suffer emotionally about someone injuring you, long after the physical injury has healed.)

Here is a good fictitious (although common) example: A daughter screams "I hate you!" to her mother. The hearing of these patterns of sounds does not hurt the mother. But it does not end there; the mother may *secondarily* think and believe "She's being hurtful," and *that* is a very painful thought to entertain and empower! This thought *about* the event is a mind-read, and it *itself*, believed in, is directly what causes the pain.

The daughter has done the same thing. She has taken outside circumstances or events, believed a painful thought into her experience, and is expressing that pain. *Her* pain, *her* hate. She is suffering.

Whether or not the daughter actually intended to be hurtful is irrelevant to the cause of the mother's pain. When you really get this, you can stop believing these thoughts, and better yet you can stop believing that the outside can hurt you. You can find compassion in the intimate knowing that we all suffer the same, and that it does not have to be this way.

So what can the mother do? As you will learn later, the best way to end someone else's suffering is to end your own. Deal with yourself first. Holding a hurtful thought is unkind. Detach from needing her to treat you kindly, and become self-fulfilling with kindness and in that way, *you* become the kind person you expect your daughter to be. The change in you will speak volumes beyond what could be said verbally to her. It takes two to tango, and when you change your part, when you change the dance, those around you must change.

GOOD INTENTIONS DON'T MATTER

On the flip side of intentional hurting, you may take action thinking that what you are doing is right. Like telling someone what they should think, or how they should feel or respond, or not. But no matter how much you truly believe you are doing what's right, you have only taken *your* beliefs, desires, hopes, fears, and mind-reads into account, and have not taken the other person into account.

"But my intentions are good!" is the common objection and rationalization or excuse, perhaps eventually followed by the angry judgment: "They just don't see. It's their problem, not mine."

However good they are, good intentions do not release you from the outcome of your actions. This became glaringly obvious to me one morning, when I awoke with a very clear message in my head:

Your intention does not matter. The effect *on others does.*

How powerful! How true. How humbling. Instantly I saw that intention = ego*, self, and separation, and that this separation is suffering. My intention means "I am deciding this should be your experience, your response."

In NLP we state it this way: "The meaning of the communication (or action) is the response it gets." In reality, the *response* is what matters—not my intention. And there is no reason why my intention and their response should be the same. *Their response is my experience too,* so I saw that I had a vested interest in caring more about the response than my intention, for myself. Seeing how this works, I began to crave "connection," or alignment with others.

As long as you keep plowing through life and people with good intentions born from your bad feelings, fears, or hopes, you will trigger hurt and never know true openness, intimacy, and love, nor your true strength to let people live their own lives. After all, you desire that for yourself, right?

When we combine a desire for an end result of love, joy, or connection, with the awareness that the only thing that matters is the other person's response—we can drop everything else, including the "rightness" of our intention (which does not bring the desired results or mutual experience anyway).

{ The road to hell is paved with good intentions. ~ Karl Marx }

Wanting the end of separation, I began to drop my own intentions and to seek, know, and allow the authentic and genuine truth of others. I did not want to hurt anyone anymore, and I did not want to hurt myself anymore. I began to yearn for *true* love and intimacy with others; beyond need, beyond what I had known before. Somehow I wanted to cross the chasm. I wanted to meet them in their place with love, instead of defiantly standing in mine with pain—and that became my quest.

Knowing that it is feeling which motivates us, and that bad feeling taints our actions, I recognized the source of my actions that hurt others was my own pain. Theoretically, if we didn't feel pain, we would not inflict pain. When did I feel pain?—when the "I" in me, the ego*, felt hurt.

The root cause of suffering is said to be this thing called "ego*"—this "ego" thing that tries to make itself separate by being more or less than someone else, this ego that needs to come first, and to protect itself at all costs—even at the cost of pain in others.

In order that I would not feel pain and therefore not inflict pain, it became my highest goal to eliminate ego. Pretty lofty! How can you eliminate something you don't understand and can't even see, feel, or find? The only thing I could come up with at the time was to put others first. That would subdue the ego! Right?

So I considered what emotion would motivate me to put others first, and what I came up with was compassion for *their* suffering.

BEING OTHER-CENTERED

Nurturing awareness of other people's suffering did a few things. For one, I stopped assuming it was "all about me." For example, if someone was upset, angry, or hurt, then instead of reacting in kind or defensively, I would ask if they were okay.

To my shock (and often to theirs), that simple question, just attending with interest to their state, instantly dissipated their emotion. That left space to learn about things they felt were upsetting them—and *it was never me!* I was in their presence, sensing and experiencing their emotion, *but it had nothing to do with me.*

Asking if someone was okay instead of feeling attacked and assuming it was about me, *made* it about them, for them and me—a complete reversal of experience.

{ Nothing people do is because of you, it is because of themselves.
~ Don Miguel Ruiz, *The Four Agreements* }

Eventually I noticed that even if I did not feel pain, my actions (or inactions) could still appear to trigger it in others. After all it is their own mind-reads that trigger their pain. (Knowing that, at least now I could have compassion, and not feel responsible.)

I did notice that I could not feel my own suffering quite as well when I was trying to feel someone else's*. So when I found myself dropping into my own suffering, I tried feeling others' suffering as an antidote. But it was just more, different suffering. Also, there wasn't always someone around suffering for me to focus on.

That was all before I knew what compassion really was, and that I can't feel someone else's suffering; but more on these later.

WHAT IS GOING ON HERE?

All this searching, re-searching and soul searching did not bring me any closer to the final, fundamental inner transformation I sought, which I began to call "Alchemy," but it did make one thing crystal clear: there was much more going on here than meets the usual mind—and thank God for that, because the tiny being I was pretending to be was becoming too claustrophobic.

Chapter 5

Inversion

{ What lies behind us and what lies before us are tiny matters compared to what lies within us. ~ Ralph Waldo Emerson }

Somehow I knew the answer was not "outside" me, because seeking answers outside me or seeking to control the outside had only ever resulted in suffering, and the outside is always changing! It's completely unreliable. During my quest for answers I noticed that all great spiritual teachers past and present have directed us to look inside.

{ Remember, the entrance door to the sanctuary is inside you.
~ Rumi }

{ What you are, the world is. And without your transformation, there can be no transformation of the world. ~ J. Krishnamurti }

{ Those who have not found their true wealth, which is the radiant joy of Being and the deep, unshakable peace that comes with it, are beggars, even if they have great material wealth. They are looking outside for scraps of pleasure or fulfillment, for validation, security, or love, while they have a treasure within that not only includes all those things but is infinitely greater than anything the world can offer.
~ Eckhart Tolle }

For about six years after Dad's passing, I looked for the path*
to inner transformation through courses and reading self-help
books, but it was through questioning and the close study of my
own direct experience that understandings came.

One day, while I was crying on the kitchen floor, my cat came
up to me and licked my nose, and that made me laugh. I thought,
"Stop it, I can't laugh. I'm suffering here!" With that little break
in state, I noticed the absurdity of this statement and laughed
harder! Then I noticed that I was suffering alone, in no one's
presence, for no reason. One moment I was fine and the next I
was crying in pain. So, what, on the "outside," was causing it now?
There was no one and nothing to blame. In that moment, I clearly
knew the source of my peace or suffering was inside! I could
never fully blame the outside again.

As it was, life brought me numerous opportunities to face
and deal with my inner suffering—the very same suffering we all
have experienced at times. In bad situations with people, I was
highly aware that I wanted something else, something different. I
wanted the exact opposite experience with them. I wanted to turn
it around into love, for them and me, and I sensed that love was
not far away*…but I did not know how to reach it*. My heart grew
more humble and tender, and began to crack open. As well, my
desire to give love and trigger only love, grew.

SEE THE SUFFERING

Looking inward, something shifted and I began to refuse to blame
anything or anyone outside for my pain. Because I held many limiting beliefs, the struggle not to blame was challenging at first. But
I was relentless and steadfast in my determination not to judge
anyone, not to form negative beliefs about others, not to blame
anyone. *Every* time that I did not, I felt better than when I did, so
I had incentive to persist.

As I lay in bed in the throes of pain and suffering, I would suddenly "see" it, the suffering, as separate from me and I knew that it was not what I wanted. Once, suddenly seeing it, I burst out laughing in the midst of crying. Something about seeing suffering seemed absurd, as was the realization that I had not seen it before. And why not?

We exist as the "knower" of experience, before all experience. Perhaps that is why it is funny. You must exist first, in order to experience what comes second, so how suffering could "sneak up" on us and then suddenly be seen is funny to me.

No matter what you are experiencing, it is not you. That is how you can know it, and see it as separate, and stop giving it the power of your attention.

Because I did not want suffering (for myself or others), I was more mindful of when it arose. Eventually I would see suffering just as it would begin to grow. Thoughts began to drop, mid-sentence. More and more often, I caught such thoughts earlier and earlier, in more and more contexts, and in ever more subtle ways.

Later, I would also notice suffering trying to raise its ugly head while I sat working or driving, or as I cleaned house. While I began to see it more often, it still seemed I could not control it or choose how I felt, until one day, during another intense episode of suffering in my life, I realized we actually do have the power; there is something we can do, a practice that anyone can use to reclaim their power.

CHAPTER 6

How the Alchemy of Love and Joy Was Born

How did this practice come to me?
I loved someone more than I loved my "self."

Saying I loved someone more than my "self" * says everything
about me and nothing at all about that person. Some "thing" had
shifted. I wanted only love and compassion. I wanted only to feel
good about people and to have them only feel good about me. It
may be that for the first time, I loved to the very Being, to the very
essence of another—beyond personality, beyond quirks, to infin-
ity. I began to love *love itself.* I became consumed by love itself and
began to desire and value love far more than I valued the sense
and experience of my egoic self*, which I realized always carried a
bad feeling in the gut and left a bad taste in the mouth.

I began to crave true, genuine, beyond boundaries intimacy—
and somehow I knew that love was the way*. That sounds pretty
funny to me now because today it is so clear to me that love is not
the "way" —love *is* it, period.

Much of my life I had always been what most people considered a positive, happy, independent, and easygoing person.
I certainly never considered myself "needy." However, like the
majority of people in our society, I was attached to needing others
for my happiness. Hook, line, and sinker, I bought the idea that
others "make" us happy. With that bait swallowed, we must also
buy the idea that others can make us unhappy. That I was unhappy

is an understatement, but the message of this book is that outer circumstances—what happens to us—does not ultimately matter. In keeping with this, I will stay focused on that message, rather than the details of that "suffering story."

The stories we carry and relive are not the past; they are actually in the now. If the past has any power or life now it is because we give it power—now. Therefore, I do not carry them, nor do I repeat them, unless for a higher purpose (and then it is not a suffering story, it is a transcending story). Yes, something happened that most people would feel I would be "justified" in suffering over. That story is no different from any other person's attachment story of suffering. It seems we have all been there. What was different this time is what happened in the middle of that suffering. Mind had plenty of "proof" that I should suffer, but for the first time, I denied mind.

Even though I felt intensely anguished, judged, abandoned, unloved, and devoid of human acceptance and dignity at that point in my life, because of love and my intention to love, for the first time I refused to hurt another, either through my words in their presence, or through my energy, thoughts, and feelings in their absence. I refused to blame anyone, judge anyone, make up beliefs about anyone, or otherwise stain anyone.

Looking for understanding, meaning, something to grasp onto, and also seeking relief, I noticed that it was "I" who felt pain with absolutely every "staining" thought that arose about another. So I rejected them all. To tarnish someone creates separation and pain. I did not want that for myself or anyone.

Giving and having only unconditional love meant to accept others' choices, thoughts, beliefs, and actions with love, even if these apparently affected me negatively*. To truly do that, I had to have zero tolerance for blaming anything or anyone outside of me for how I felt. These choices—no, these decisions—forced me to take one-hundred-percent responsibility for what I felt, forced me to find the truth about the cause of what I feel, and forced me to detach from needing the outside*. Since blaming, which was my usual way out of a painful experience up until then, was no longer an option, I went inside, deeply inside.

There were intense weeks of pain and suffering. I had put myself in a box with no known way out. My mind whirled like a tornado. I did not want things to be as they were, but they were as they were. "How could this be?" and "This should not be" were thoughts that fueled the funnel to spin faster and faster, higher and higher. Everything tossed in was shattered into shards that ripped and tore me up inside. "I want" was the deadliest, most painful, and most futile thought, yet it was also the one that pointed out the reality that, in fact, I did not have what I wanted and no matter how badly "I wanted" in my mind, no matter how much I suffered in that moment, reality was not going to change.

Then, both by desperately seeking relief and wanting to give love no matter what, the box exploded. I came to an end. I did not want to suffer any more. But I did not just "not want" to suffer, for me suffering was no longer an option. Just like blaming was no longer an option. Realizing and clearly seeing that suffering does not change anything, for a brief moment, not knowing what else to do, I just stopped. In this fleeting moment of stillness I knew or remembered or heard, "You can give yourself whatever you want." Then the pain began to build again and in the middle of intense suffering, I wondered, "Well, even if that were true, what *do* I want?"

At the time, there were a lot of things: acceptance, connection, dignity and respect, and mostly love, true love. If you can give yourself what you want, then it does not come from the outside; so I pulled my attention from the outside. Then it happened.

Instead of putting my attention on what I didn't want and what I didn't have and on the outside, I went inside and looked for everything I *did* want—*and they were there!* All of the intense energy that was being used to feel bad flipped over into feeling good. And then it flipped back. But I had caught glimpse of it— whoa!—*what was that?*

I looked for them again, and again they were there! In the middle of unwanted outside circumstances, in the middle of my suffering, I found immediate joy: a complete and radical reversal of feeling in the moment. Instantly, happiness blossomed and immense pleasure began to fill my body from everywhere, all at once. Seeking the acceptance I wanted, it was there, as was the connection, respect, dignity, and even love. One by one, I recognized them all and basked in ever-expanding happiness, peace, and joy. This was so simple, yet radically powerful!

At first it seemed hard to believe, yet there it was: joy. Then I thought maybe it would not last, but it was such a relief, so I kept my attention there. Then I thought that maybe this type of reversal could not be repeated. But I had been hurting so much for so long, and I wanted to feel good more than I wanted the outside to change (which was not changing, regardless, anyway), that I held it and it stayed, repeated, and settled in.

What I have come to call "old-mind" did battle with me for a few weeks and habitual thoughts arose like, "But you can't feel good because of this (outside) "reality," and you certainly can't feel joyful!" Yet in spite of my circumstances, I did. "But I *AM* feeling it!" was the indisputable answer. Having discovered this inner joy, I put my attention on it and ignored thoughts about the outside. Experiencing them both at the same time destroyed my belief that I had to feel bad.

At times there was flip-flopping between automatic, habitual suffering and feeling good, but I persisted in seeking good feeling, again and again. When a bad feeling was noticed, I would seek what *was* wanted; I would seek the opposite good feeling. I would seek joy. "Seeing" the suffering arise and causing joy right in the middle of it made me spontaneously burst out laughing. That experience was funny, and so was knowing the *powerlessness* of the outside world to affect me inside. It was tremendously freeing.

With each experience of transcending old-mind, the already deeply wounded habit of believing old-mind was being eradicated. In spite of the old beliefs that passed by as thoughts, joy persisted as my predominant state, irrelevant to words and thought, and separate from my circumstances. This was all done directly through feeling; I had no words for it.

Revelations began to come. I had been feeling the pain of not having acceptance, connection, respect, and love because I had been denying them to myself. Like a hidden treasure, underneath all the pain, the joy was always there. I had discovered that we *are* either "being-feeling good" or we *are* "being-feeling bad." It is that simple and direct. There are no other reasons for pain or joy.

PAIN CONCEDES TO PLEASURE

As I began consciously to seek and use good feeling, positive thoughts, sounds, and pictures began to arise. I kept, held, and nurtured whatever felt good, rejecting everything else. The relief kept me returning for more. Then I took this approach one step further; I began doing it not just to relieve pain, but to actively seek pleasure.

After any pain subsided in my experience, I grew the pleasure by maintaining my attention on what I wanted. By enjoying and appreciating the good feeling, I noticed it grew larger and larger. The moments when I consciously took time to create and enjoy feeling good I began to call "Feel Good Fests." During these fests, I stopped whatever I was doing, went to the same place (my bed or a certain chair), snuggled into it, felt into the body, and reached for and nurtured a better feeling, allowing it to grow.

This became something I really looked forward to, like a hot bath or any other peaceful or fun habitual activity. Soon, the moment I moved toward the bed or chair, I also began to feel good with anticipation. This is the opposite of what one might do when feeling bad, which would be going to the bedroom to cry. Rather than the habit of seeking "the reasons" I felt bad, it was time to stop, pay attention, go inside, and seek what *was* wanted. Feeling bad meant it was time to feel good!

~

The old thoughts lost more power every day, and simultaneously in inverse proportion, the most amazing joy arose in their place. About two weeks before the practice that I now call *The Alchemy of Love and Joy*™ came to me, something was building, forming, or being created in me, as I continued to experience this loss and gain. I knew and sensed something was emerging, but I did not know what. Friends noted that my energy was "on overdrive." But with no words to explain it, how could I share it?

It had not yet coalesced into something I could verbalize when I went to a friend's place to brainstorm on her business. Arriving pumped with happiness, immediately, I knew something was bothering her and asked what was up.

As she began to share, it was as if I had been transported back to my point of breakthrough and yet was at the same time present with her and her pain, highly aware and keenly alert, and remembering...then words in the form of questions flowed from me to her. To both of our surprise, her feeling, her energy, her thoughts, and her resourcefulness around the issue shifted on the spot.

Wide-eyed with amazement, I looked at my friend, as realization of what just happened dawned on me. *What had worked for me had worked for her. And these were the words!*

"I'm sorry," I said. "We can't start yet; I need to write this down." Inside I was bursting. It felt like intense energy was sparking through my every cell, and my whole body tingled. Goose bumps broke out. I scrambled fast to capture the questions on paper for fear of losing any one of them, mumbling, "That's it, that's *it!*"

My friend, still processing her shift and what happened, listened as I blabbered what I could about what I had been experiencing since discovering this power of love and joy, and how I knew that something wanted to emerge, but that I had no idea what—and that *this was it!*

Since I was there to work for my friend, I felt torn. I wanted to help her and I also did not want to stifle the gift that was emerging, so I kept saying, "I'll work on it later." But by that time, she was into it, and began asking me questions.

I described my radical shifts from suffering to joy, including details of how the pain of suffering awakened me to seek joy, how I learned I could trigger and "call" joy whenever I want to, how my senses became heightened and the whole world seemed shiny and new again, and how I began to notice the pleasure in simply breathing. I described how, later, I had experienced blissful, ecstatic moments that arose while just appreciating life and the aliveness within and around me. Everything I had been experiencing, yet had been unable to verbalize until then, exploded into colorful, ethereal words and excitement.

They thought I had been on overdrive? We hadn't seen anything yet. That was a Monday. By Friday, I had the practice created, the book written, designed, and printed, and a website published. Unable to stop, I was driven to share this story and *Alchemy*, staying up until one, two, and three in the morning each night. There was no way I could not share, as fast as I could, this so simple, yet radical and immensely powerful end to suffering. Yet the end of mental suffering was just the beginning. What I discovered beyond relief is deliciously delightful. Now I live almost predominantly in pleasure, happiness, joy, relaxation, or excitement—and in peace with *all* that is and with *all* that is not.

It became increasingly difficult for me to see things as "good" or "bad." All is as it is. All can be loved as it is. Thoughts now bring me peace. The expanded sense of being has altered my experience of everything; resulting in anything from appreciation to intense ecstasy for even the simplest of things. My senses have awakened to taste, sight, sound, smell, touch, and feeling in an innocent, pure, childlike way.

These are some of the fringe benefits that come from recognizing the false causes of suffering and realizing the true source of joy through *Alchemy*, which you can learn to use.

CHAPTER 7

Using the Alchemy of Love and Joy

Alchemy is a fundamental, irreversible change like transforming lead into gold. For me the word signified the complete reversal of my inner experience and my outer response to others.

There was a scene in a movie where a young man was telling his mother that not only was he not going to marry the woman of *her* dreams, but he was "going away with" a woman of the "wrong" status, the "wrong" ethnicity, *and* the "wrong" religion. This was unthinkable in their country at the time. His mother experienced intense shock, suffering, and anger.

Yet even through her rage he was not scared, hurt, or upset. Instead of feeling rejected and unloved, in the middle of his mother's pain, *his love* and compassion for *her* was obvious. In that way, the situation was all about *her*, not about him or his choices. As a result, the scene did not become one of argument or anger. It did not take long for his mother to connect with her love for him. Angst gave way to motherly love, and then concern for him.

That was how I wanted to be, no matter what. While I did not know how, I sensed it was possible and was inspired to discover the cause of suffering so I could be fundamentally free, for myself and others.

The cause of psychological suffering

What I experientially discovered is that we don't need people, places, or things. You are complete and whole as you are, and you are all you will ever need. The action of believing you need something outside of you is, *itself*, what causes dissatisfaction.

The pain of suffering is caused by wanting or not wanting. When we are *wanting* something, we are actually experiencing the lack of something. To experience yourself as less than complete is painful.

On top of that, we struggle against reality, which hurts. We are either feeling what is wanted (which feels good) or we are feeling the *wanting* (which feels bad). Both experiences are always optional and available no matter what is going on around you. Let's use feeling disrespected to illustrate this.

Disrespect

Even when you don't want something, you want something, and again you are feeling the lack of something (that you do want). You can prove this now. For example, let's say that you don't want to feel "disrespected." How does *not* feeling "disrespected" feel? In other words, what *do* you want instead? Maybe it is respect? Is that what you want? How does being respected feel?

Take some time. Words like "valued" and "considered" may come to mind. Allow only whatever supports the feeling of respect to come while you stay *laser focused* on the good feeling you do want. How does being respected feel? Go into it. Feel into your body for the answer. Answer it *with* your body. See it, hear it, feel it. Fully enjoy it.

Notice…you are feeling it *now*.

Did you need anyone else to give it to you?

Is this what you prefer to feel?

Who's respect did you need?

You might notice it was your own.

Feeling this way, how do you act?

Feeling this way, you probably *anticipate* respect, *communicate* respect, and respectfully *require* respect. When you feel respect, you respect yourself and others, don't you?

You know how you used to act when not feeling respected. How much more likely will *feeling* respected (and therefore acting respected), get you (outer) respect?

Is that what you prefer to do?

Not feeling respected means it is time to give respect to yourself. It is time to *feel* respect. You do not require A, B, or C to happen outside of you in order for you to know and feel respect inside, or in order for you to be the respectable person you are.

CONNECTION

This is so universally common that I am going to cover it in depth here. What if your partner wants intimacy, but you are not feeling connected? Feeling disconnected, how do you act?

What do you do? Not respond? Pull away? Act disconnected? How would acting disconnected get you the connection you want? How do you think your partner might interpret your actions and feel? How does that get you the connection you want? It doesn't, right? Not feeling connected, you might wait for your partner to do the thing that you believe would "make" you feel connected. But what if it did not happen? Would you feel angry or hurt? Then what would you do, and how would that get you the connection you wanted? Is that what you prefer to have and to give to your partner?

What if you just went inside and gave it to yourself first?

Ask yourself: "What do I want?"

If you answer, "I want to feel connected," ask yourself, "How does feeling connected feel?"

Take all the time you need to go into it deeply, feeling for how being connected feels. Feel through your whole body as you see connection, hear connection, and feel and sense connection. Experience it in as many ways as possible. Really enjoy connection.

Then ask yourself: "Is this what I prefer to feel?

"Who did I need to feel connected?"

"Who's connection did I really need?"

Now ask, "Feeling connected, how do I act?"

How might your partner feel about your actions now? What could happen now? How good could the connection really get?

Ask yourself: "Is this what I prefer to do, give, or project?"

Not feeling connected means it is time to give connection to yourself. It is time to *feel* connected.

PEACE

What if you didn't want someone else to feel anxious?

Ask: "What do I want?"

Perhaps you want them to feel calm and peaceful.

Ask yourself: "How does them feeling calm and peaceful feel?"

Again, answer it bodily. Go deeply into it, notice how your body responds. Perhaps it releases and relaxes as it becomes calm and peaceful. See, hear, feel, and know what calm and peaceful are like.

Now ask yourself, "Is this what I prefer to feel?"

"Who did I need to feel calm and peaceful?"

Now ask, "Feeling this way, how do I act?"

Perhaps you project calm, peaceful energy, or share calm thoughts or clear, creative ideas. Your calming demeanor helps another to stay grounded and be more resourceful.

Then ask, "Is this what I prefer to do?"

Now you can see one aspect of the non-separation of you and others: what you feel, you get and have. What you have, you offer. What you offer, you see "reflected" in others.

LOVE IN ABSENCE

Think of someone alive whom you care about and who is not there. And ask yourself:

"What do I want?"

Maybe it's to have them there.
Ask: "How does them being here feel?"

Feeling them here, see, hear, know that feeling. Scan up and down your body for the good feeling. Take your time and enjoy the good feeling, happiness, and sensations.

Then at the peak, ask: "Is this what I prefer feel?"
    "Who's presence did I need?"
    "Feeling this way, how do I act?"

Maybe you clean the place or go buy a surprise gift for their return, or maybe you give them a friendly call. Now ask: "Is this what I prefer to do, share, give…or project?"

(I am not responsible for what happens next, though I do suggest you "send" it to them.) You can lie there, feeling what it's like to miss someone, feeling lack or feeling sorry for yourself, or you can enjoy and appreciate the feeling of their presence. The only separation that exists is the one you choose to feel. Connection, love, and joy are always available to you.

DECEASED LOVED ONE

Again, you can experience missing them, or you can experience some other good feeling. Either feeling will be equally real at the time. Pick a feeling, perhaps the love of someone who has passed.

Now ask yourself: "How does their love feel?"

Really tap in, see it, hear it, and feel their love. Keeping your attention on it, take your time to savor and enjoy it. Appreciating it and then enjoying it more, build it to a peak.

Now ask yourself: "Is this what I prefer to feel?
    "Who did I need?"
    "Feeling this way, how do I act?"

Maybe you…"send" it to them!

Now ask yourself, "Is this what I prefer to share, give, or project?"

> { If, instead of a gem or even a flower, we would cast the gift
> of a lovely thought into the heart of a friend, that would be
> giving as angels give. ~ George MacDonald }

WITH JOY COMES INSIGHT

Since joy came to me, clarity and many more understandings have also been coming. How did joy truly come to me? You know the outside story, but the inner truth of how it came to me is that it never left. It is and has always been here as an ability from birth, for all of us.

I came to know that "not wanting to suffer" *is* suffering—and that I needed to remain laser-focused on the good feeling that *was* wanted. The more I practiced, the more happiness and joy I felt; the more I wanted it, the more I practiced. Then another realization came:

You cannot give love while you are suffering.

Which do you want to experience?
Which do you want to give?

WHAT YOU WANT IS RIGHT

When answering "What do I want?" old-mind and thoughts might try to slip in to judge your answer. People sometimes don't like (i.e. they judge) certain desires that gave birth to a bad feeling, and so they may lie to themselves. Instead, be brutally honest so you can discover the truth because it does set you free.

Rest assured that the deeper purpose is always positive. Know that what you want to feel is always right. Is it attention? Is it to feel important? To feel part of what's going on? Whatever it is, it's okay. Allow it.

You are a part of this whole universe and it is your inherent right to feel you belong—or any other way you like. It is your right to feel important, connected, happy, valued, and so forth. What has not been right, perhaps, nor effective, was the way you went about trying to get it: (1) from the outside; and then, because you believed the outside held it, (2) especially through manipulating the outside (an impossible task, anyway).

You don't need to look outwards. There is much love for you, here, right now. First give it fully to yourself inside and all things will right themselves outside.

{ I don't need your approval, I need mine. ~ Byron Katie }

THE ESSENCE OF ALCHEMY

When we are *wanting* something, we have taken something away from ourselves, something that was already there—and *is always* there. That is why we can "give" it back, and using *Alchemy* is how.

Unlike the ever-changing, uncontrollable outside, that which you can give yourself is more reliable than anything outside. It is eternally available. (After all, you are always with yourself).

The questions presented in this chapter are the ones that came through me for my friend, and they reflect the non-verbal shift of attention and feeling that happened inside me when I discovered the power of love and joy. But the questions themselves, of course, are not the solution to suffering.

Doing the practice is the actual recognizing and reaching for any missed feeling. It is how you can give yourself anything you want, now.

JOY IS NOT GAINED

I say you can "give" yourself what you want but this happens by shifting your attention onto what was always available, so actually, joy is not gained, it is only recognized. You can use *Alchemy* to return to your wholeness and detach from wanting anything outside so you can know eternal love and peace.

When you look at and experience the whole of reality (as it is), and feel good or at peace while facing some apparently "adverse" condition on the outside, you can know with conviction that nothing outside of you can hurt you. You can drop that fundamental belief. This freedom from the attachment of needing the outside is not something you gain; it's the shedding of the shackles of "self."

{ You don't need anything to be happy. You need something to be unhappy. ~ Mooji, quoting his teacher Papaji }

Your natural state is joy, peace, and love. To experience anything else, you must have something else "added" that blinds you to them; you must have a reason or a belief that you must suffer. The *idea* that you need something or someone to be happy is what keeps you unhappy. Without belief in that thought, you can know the peace that is always already there. You can know the freedom that you inherently already are.

The practice of *The Alchemy of Love and Joy*™ can be used as a remedy for suffering in the moment, to realize freedom, and to know and enjoy joy. Astoundingly, as I have experientially learned, it can also be used for expansion of knowing and presence of being. First, let's look closer at what reality and knowing are.

WHAT IS REALITY?

When "feeling a loved one" who is absent, one of the objections slippery old-mind might offer is something like, "Yeah, but it's not *real*; he or she is not here." This statement is evidence of mistaking the person for the feeling. The feeling is real and does not require anyone else's presence but your own. Have you ever been beside someone and felt alone, disconnected, or sad? Someone being there does not guarantee a good feeling, as I am sure you know. So someone not being there cannot be the cause of feeling bad, either. This false mass belief is incongruent, yet it is often used to support suffering.

When doing the practice and answering, "How does having that person here feel?" and connecting with the feeling, is the good feeling in your body real? In your *experience*? Is the good feeling any less real than the bad feeling? Who made the good feeling? Who made the bad feeling? Who did you need to be there?

Whether you are with someone or alone, the source of pain or joy is only within you. Your beliefs and where you put your attention dictate your experience.

Not only that—do you know that we never directly experience "reality;" that our experience, the delivery of sensory information from our biology and nervous system to the brain, is always *behind* reality, actually slower than the event? This body-mind takes time to process things, and more mind-boggling yet, the brain is playing tricks on our senses, for a higher purpose.

YOUR BRAIN MANUFACTURES YOUR REALITY

Different sense impulses like touch, sight, and sound travel at different speeds in the body. For example, a toe-touch signal takes longer to reach the brain than a touch to other parts of the body. In his book *Brain Time*, David M. Eagleman, neuroscience Ph.D., says that

{ ...the system waits to collect information over the window of time during which it streams in....If I touch your toe and your nose at the same time, you will feel those touches as simultaneous. This is surprising, because the signal from your nose reaches your brain well before the signal from your toe. Why didn't you feel the nose-touch when it first arrived? Did your brain wait to see what else might be coming up in the pipeline of the spinal cord until it was sure it had waited long enough for the slower signal from the toe? Strange as that sounds, it may be correct. [...]...snap your fingers in front of your face. The sight of your fingers and the sound of the snap appear simultaneous. But it turns out that impression is laboriously constructed by your brain. }

In essence, your brain manufactures your perception of reality. Eagleman points out that during the invention of television "...engineers worried about the problem of keeping audio and video signals synchronized." But they discovered that there was about a hundred milliseconds of room for error: "As long as the signals arrived within this window, viewers' brains would automatically resynchronize the signals," he wrote.

So just what is reality? Is it when your toe is touched, or when the signal reaches the brain? Or when the brain assimilates it? As you can see, "reality" is not absolute, and that is just the beginning. Beyond the biology of the senses, when all this hits the mind, even what we conclude about the experience is not actual reality itself; it is our *perception* of the experience.

If you liked the person who touched your foot, your "reality" or experience would be different than if you disliked them. We run thoughts about what happens on the outside through the filters of our expectations, beliefs, anticipations, fears, and hopes *inside*—and *before* we decide on a feeling to have—before *we decide* what our experience will be and what reality is for us.

Experience does not happen "out there." We thought what we experienced was "out there," which is impossible. All we feel, sense, see, hear, and experience is done *in here*—where we choose the meaning!

That's actually good news, because it means reality has always been, and always is, whatever we individually make it. Sometimes we experience what we have been unconsciously conditioned to experience, other times what we conditioned ourselves to experience, and sometimes what we have consciously chosen. You can override conditioning, and you can change your conditioning.

> *Experience is not what happens to us.*
> *It is how we choose to feel about things that happen.*

Joyful experiences are as "real" as any other experience, and they positively affect the body-mind. Even if you are not suffering, there is value in engaging in them. Knowing joy in your life will prevent all manner of mental confusion, stress, and physical illness. It will motivate and inspire you, enable you to take resourceful action, to be strong for others, and to contribute. It will also enable you to expand beyond the fears and limits that have restricted you in the past.

You are invited to look deeply into your direct experience, and to closely notice and then question your assumptions and unconscious beliefs. Come along with me and engage life as an adventure again. Become curious and begin to explore the "limits" and you will come to know that there aren't any, and that there is always more. You are capable of much more joy than you have lived—*or imagined!*

CHAPTER 8

Is This All There Is to Life?

No!

You are capable of much more joy than you have lived—or imagined, and in fact, your imagination is what has kept you from it.

> { If we could see the miracle of a single flower clearly,
> our whole life would change. ~ Buddha }

As a young child, standing in front of and staring in awe at a massive tree, you experience it from a point of purity and innocence. The escorting adult, amused by your awe, and well-intentioned, interrupts your experience with, "That's a *tree*." You stop, turn, look up, and mouth "tree," and are rewarded with the smile you've learned you can feel good about. Now you experience the label "tree"—and no longer the tree itself. And it's not the same.

Then you learn to describe the tree. You learn "green" and you begin to "see" the label green—and no longer the rich depths, variations, or shades and hues of *living,* changing green.

> { I don't trust concepts, I only trust awareness. ~ Ajahn Sumedho }

How many different shades of green are there? An infinite number! But we have only several labels, which are thoughts. Direct experience has been dulled-over by simple, boring labels that were only intended to serve as maps in order to describe and attempt to communicate experience.

{ The map is not the territory. ~ NLP presupposition }

The tendency to label can distance you from your life because you then experience the label, not life. Compared to the vast and vibrant richness of the direct experience of life, labels are ordinary. So living and knowing labels, thoughts, instead of the miracle of actual experience, everything in life becomes "ordinary."

Dropping labels and putting attention back onto direct experience, you will find you are capable of much more pleasure and joy than you have experienced or imagined. There is nothing ordinary about what is going on here, and you will know that when you look at, or contact, this miracle directly.

{ There are no ordinary moments.
~ Dan Millman, *Way of the Peaceful Warrior* }

When we suffer we try to shut down and shut out our experience. Once you begin to end suffering and practice feeling the alive energy in this body, then feeling good, then joy, and doing this more and more habitually in your life, it is similar to being born brand-new. You once again experience life from innocence, from not knowing: without thought to get between you and life.

LIMITLESS PLEASURE, BEYOND BELIEF

As beliefs, thoughts, and labels that used to cloud experience drop, simple things in life "come to life" as though you had never seen them before. When you see the miracle of the sheer existence of reality, when you directly and wordlessly contemplate the mystery with awe and appreciation, then the brightness intensifies and the sharpness magnifies—raising your enjoyment. Leaving limiting thought and labels, being in the present moment and practicing joy awakens and appears to enhance all the senses. More accurately, it frees them to see with clarity that which was already the case.

This body, this life, is a great mystery; a great gift awaiting the curious who will acknowledge it as such and unwrap it. How good you can feel, how vibrant something can look, how flavorful something can taste, how fantastic something can sound, how ecstatic intimacy can be, and even simply how your body feels has been limited by belief and predominant attention on thought.

When you begin to notice feeling good in the face of adversity, then, using any of its endless reasons, the mind may suggest that you can't feel good. No matter what, practice allowing the acknowledgement of *feeling,* because we have believed our thoughts over our actual experience for far too long. Believe the senses—whether you are feeling good, or then feeling better, or feeling great, or feeling more and more ecstatic—believe the actual experience—not the thought about what you "should or should not" or "can or cannot" be feeling. Believe the experience, and if you are going to believe any thought, then like I did when pain was transcended by joy, let it be "but I *AM* feeling it!"

You can know so much greater sensual and joyful heights in the whole of your experience. It's as if a dull fog lifts and life becomes the joyous, sensational adventure that it is. You may begin to wonder, as I have, just how good life can get as you continually meet the expansiveness that is your own. Become an adventurer; question all you thought you knew, and you will begin to notice the miracle in everything, even in the sheer existence of the simplest things. Your life will come alive!

{ There are only two ways to live your life. One is as though
nothing is a miracle. The other is as though everything is a miracle.
~ Albert Einstein }

At one point during a "Feel Good Fest" I wondered, "Just how much pleasure could someone have?" Well, the answer is as much as the suffering that we can have, or more! I found there was no limit, except in a belief that there was a limit! Feel into your body. There is life in it. And life is alive, pleasurable. Life is love. Feel into your body, feel into love.

WHAT'S YOUR UPPER LIMIT?

Just as we can believe we must suffer to a certain degree, we have beliefs that we can only feel "so good." These beliefs, which are just habitual thoughts, must be continually re-thought, and re-proven; supported by "evidence," or they dissolve. So we experience much suffering, and we experience limited joy in order to prove we can only feel "so good" because there is one thing the mind cannot stand: incongruence between reality and beliefs. Perceived reality and our beliefs *must* match. So if we are not willing to question our beliefs, we sabotage good feeling in order to remain congruent.

You can prove to yourself that you have "only so good" beliefs by taking a few quiet minutes and admiring a plant that you like. When you notice a good feeling, enjoy that for a few minutes, and then feel gratitude and appreciation for that feeling *itself*.

What happened? Feeling expanded and grew, didn't it?

Now take that bigger feeling, and enjoy *it*.
Then appreciate it.

Continue this, alternating enjoying with feeling appreciation for the good feeling, and see what happens. See how far you can go, feeling better and better.

Most probably, at some point, a bad-feeling thought will arise such as, "Oh you can't feel *that* good!" Then what happens to the good feeling? It instantly fizzles, right? (But you *are* feeling it—until you believe you can't.) If something challenges our beliefs by opposing them in our experience, we do one of two things:

(1)   We loosen, modify, or drop the belief, or

(2)   We "delete or distort" our perception or memory of the experience in order to suit our belief.

Otherwise, there would be incongruence and our sense of "reality" would be compromised.

To know the joy, peace, and bliss you are capable of, you need to notice the limiting thoughts, but not believe them into life, by simply keeping your attention on the good feeling.

WE MUST BE CONGRUENT

Because we need to be congruent and because we have tended to mistake our beliefs (our thoughts) to *be* our selves—to be *who* we are—we can cling to them stubbornly, even to the point of warping our perception of reality to fit our beliefs! Yes, what we generally suffer over is our *perception* of reality, not reality itself.

For example, someone at work says "You cut your hair." Now, depending on your beliefs about the world in general, like whether or not people are generally well-intentioned, or your beliefs about the person speaking, you may mind-read "she hates my hair" and suffer over that thought. That thought is now your "reality," *but it is not what happened.* She did not say she hated your hair. Or, if you think the world is kind, or you like this person, you may mind-read "she likes my hair" and have a good feeling. Once again, that thought is now your inner "reality," but again, it is not what happened on the outside.

Notice that if you believe a good thought-feeling, you have a good experience of what happened. When you believe a bad thought-feeling you have a bad experience. Your experience may be either good or bad, but the outside truth of what she said is still the same, either way.

Alternatively, you realize that she simply noticed your haircut, without meaning added. In truth, you have no way of knowing her meaning or purpose for the statement, without asking her. Yet your experience can create an illusion, a false outer reality for you, if it is not true for another. This belief in your mind-read as absolute truth, is delusion.

While this is how suffering is supported, there is also good news; it means there is no inherent reality; your reality is whatever you put your attention on. This also is how two people can witness the same event and come away with completely different versions of what happened. All our individual realities are different.

You are responsible for your mind-read, no one else. Of course, even if you notice a negative mind-read thought, you don't *have* to feel bad. That would be attachment to thought, which is also an "outside" thing because it is a *known*, known *by* you. It is not you. You can notice it come, and you can notice it go, without believing it into life.

{ We give all the meaning there is to everything that happens.
~ @Deepak_Chopra, via Twitter }

88

WHAT AN EXCEPTIONAL, ECSTATIC LIFE,
WHEN YOU ARE IN THE MYSTERY, NOT "IN THE KNOW"

It is possible to not know, and still be. You know she said you cut your hair. That's it. That's all. From this point, from this perspective, just notice all the possibilities, the space, the freedom. I encourage you to become an adventurer, to challenge all your limiting beliefs, even the "good" ones. Wonder how much in life you have been missing, wonder how much more you are capable of, and just how good life, as it is, can be.

Questioning everything you thought you knew will open up new worlds, amazing possibilities, and maybe even result in "miracles." In my experience so far, I have found no limit to the degree, intensity, or frequency that I can experience joy and bliss. *No one knows how good it can get—and what joy in trying to discover!*

The benefits are unlimited, and unlike painful suffering, regular experiences of love, connection, and joy support a generally healthy and happy mind, body, and spirit. Take control of your life, your experiences, and take responsibility for your "self" and your effect "on" others' triggers and attachments. Then others cannot affect you, and yet there will be compassion, because you remember being attached and hurting, and not knowing how to stop.

{ We are all functioning at a small fraction of our capacity
to live fully in its total meaning of loving, creating and adventuring.
Consequently, the actualizing of our potential can become the most
exciting venture of our lifetime. ~ Herbert Otto }

IS THIS DENIAL?

"Is this denial?" is a question I have been asked. The answer is yes and no. Yes, it is denial of the belief that something outside can hurt you or can make you happy—and that denial will return you to sanity and peace. While you put attention on and sustain the feeling you *do* want, in spite of outside conditions and while looking directly at the conditions (not denying them), you are not denying the *totality* of your reality.

Do you want to feel better more than you want to believe old-mind? Suspend any beliefs that say this is not possible.

The reality is that there is much more available to you. There's always much more going on in your experience that is *not* suffering than is suffering. So the truth is: *suffering is denial.*

WARNING: YOU CAN BE LOST IN FEELING GOOD

You can become so narrowed, focused, and contracted on a giddy happiness that you also don't see or hear anything else in your reality. You can become lost. You can also eliminate much of reality, including what is undesired (and this is how we can wear rose-colored glasses early in relationships).

Are you present; are you aware of and feeling into your body? Are you seeing with a full range of vision? Or have you become manically narrowed because of some outside event?

What is the source of your pleasure? Is there an "object" of your pleasure? This would mean that you are still attached to the outside. Take ownership of every feeling, even the good ones!

{ They whose thoughts are of sensual objects are attached
to them, attachment gives rise to desires, and anger is born
when these desires are obstructed. ~ Bhagavad Gita }

There are Zen teachings that suggest that even happiness is suffering because you are unconscious, still attached, and will eventually come back down, perhaps even lower. And if you do get the object of your desire (including happiness itself), it will inevitably leave or change because everything changes; everything is transient, and comes and goes. The type of joy I speak of is not attached, has no object which it is happy "about," and has no cause other than your interest and attention. It is joy for no reason other than itself. It is the joy of Being.

The key is simple, and you are already doing this. In fact *you can't help but do it!*

CHAPTER 9

The Practice of Feeling

THERE ARE ONLY TWO KINDS OF FEELING

"Feelings" are not the same as "feeling." Feelings are labels for different flavors and variations of feeling; they are thoughts. You don't need to know which specific emotion you want. You don't need to mentally label them. That would be slipping into *thinking*, not feeling. There are hundreds of labels for feelings, but there are really only two kinds of feeling: bad and good. You know which one you are feeling at any time.

This is your internal guidance system, and you don't need to analyze the myriad of thoughts you are having that come with a bad feeling—all you need to do is reach for a better feeling. The thoughts, which are constantly flying and changing, will shift on their own accord when the feeling does. Once you are feeling better, clarity and access to the whole picture (which could otherwise be called intelligence), comes.

During most daily activities, we usually feel one degree or another of good or bad. Staying aware of how you feel and caring enough to feel good, relaxed, peaceful, or joyful, will habituate the positive, keep the body healthy, keep us open to intelligence, keep us consciously aware—and it just feels great!

EVERYONE FEELS

Some people believe they are numb, but even numb is a feeling. Some people believe they can't feel their emotions, or that they have stuffed their feelings "down" so far for so long that they can't "reach" them. Just exactly where is "far down"? Where have they gone that they can never arise again? Do you actually believe they are normally stored "just within reach," and that there is a place further away you can push them to but cannot again reach them? This illustrates what happens with groundless concepts, which by nature beg all kinds of questions, which themselves point out the absurdity of such concepts.

Feeling is feeling into your state in the moment, good or bad. You may attempt to dull your feeling, or otherwise modify your perception and experience of it through belief, but you are still feeling, whatever it is you are feeling. Everyone has the same billions of neurons firing through their nervous system, creating feeling, which is always available to your experience. The only people not feeling are dead people.

Trying to ignore how you feel is a defense mechanism, an attempt to protect yourself from pain. But by the time you are stuffing it, you must have already felt it! You may have come to believe that if you allow any feeling, you may suffer, so you may have decided to try to shut all feeling down, including joy. From birth, there was joy. Joy is healing, joy is love. If you have shut down joy, that *is* suffering.

The solution is not to ignore how you feel nor to stuff emotions, but to be aware of them and consciously seek what you do want. Since the world outside is always changing uncontrollably, how much safer are you when you can shift your attention and experience inside?

A belief is just a thought that you keep repeating. For example, "I can't feel it," is just another thought, believed in. Because you are not feeling it right now does not mean you cannot feel it. It means your attention is on thinking, not feeling. We feel with the body, not with a thought. In this practice you become quiet and feel into the body, head-to-toe, seeking what you want. It is there and if you persist, you will become aware of it.

In the beginning it may feel awkward, like learning to ride a bike. That is a good sign because feeling awkward does not mean you can't do something; it means you are learning something new! We are comfortable with what we already know, and learning something new feels strange or even uncomfortable for a while, until it is no longer new to us. So you are succeeding! (Note also that feeling awkward at least means *you are feeling*).

Take your time and adamantly seek the next best feeling, starting with even the smallest improvement, and you will gradually build to feeling good. There is nothing you need to trust other than the better feeling that you have in the moment, which does not need trust. You have nothing to lose but pain.

Some people try to dull bad thought-feeling with alcohol, drugs, distractions, TV, or through constantly being busy. These are outside temporary fixes that mask the opportunity to feel and learn joy—and they leave the underlying attachment and wanting intact, there to resurface again and again and again.

The ultimate control and only truly safe and peaceful place is in mastery of your self. It is also the most joyful place. Get on the bike and practice feeling how you want to and you will get there. With every gradual move toward a better and better feeling, you become more adept at knowing good feeling.

KNOWING WHAT IT'S LIKE

It may be the case, or the belief, that you have never experienced or had what it is you seek. For example, what if you've never been successful; never experienced success in your own life?

First of all, this cannot be true. Did you feel successful the first time you tied your shoes? Poured milk into a glass? Rode a bike? Also, you have ever heard about, read, or seen cases of success in friends, books, TV or movies? In seeing, hearing, or watching those experiences, you created and experienced a feeling of success inside.

Secondly, we don't want outside things, we want the feeling, so even if you have not had what you seek in your life, you do have access to the feeling you seek, or you would not be able to know *not* having it.

At first, noticing the better feeling may take you a little while, and that's okay too; with practice it will get faster and easier. Simply persist. Even persisting is not feeling bad. Because you are not focusing on what you don't want, it must also be somewhat better.

USE YOUR BODY

Your physiology is tied into your feeling, so just cracking a smile will also help, as will moving your body. If you get stuck, and you really think you don't know what you want, ask yourself: What if you did? What would it be?

WAKING AWARENESS

Another reason you may at first feel awkward or disconnected is that you are just beginning to practice awareness, or consciousness. It is possible to whip through life totally unconscious of your senses and feeling, just like being able to whip across the highway and arrive without memory of the trip. Does it mean the highway was not there?

Your mind can wander off, but your body is always present. When your attention comes back into your body there is often a feeling of relief, accompanied by a sudden release or relaxation because your body has been held captive by unconscious, automatic thought patterns (most likely negative) that held it tense or tight.

The more you practice feeling into your body, the more you practice awareness and presence, the more you will feel your emotional guidance system, which is always pointing you toward joy.

STAY WITH WHAT YOU *DO* WANT

It is utterly important to stay with the feeling of what you *do* want. Old habitual thinking may try to send you into the past, the future, into fears, disbeliefs, or objections. These are just thoughts. Simply notice and leave them alone, and they will pass.

Continually scan the body, feeling into it. Stay single-pointedly on the better feeling, reach for it, see it, hear it, feel it, no matter how small. Once you "latch" onto it this way, allow supporting positive thoughts, images, and sounds, that may come but stay with the feeling, which will grow. Once you have a "solid" enough good feeling, just bask in it, enjoy it. Simply staying with it will expand the feeling, perhaps into other larger ones like peace, satisfaction, and an overall feeling of well-being.

If at any point in doing this you notice a different bad thought-feeling beginning to arise, notice it and use the practice with *it*.

Be relentless—answer "How does [what I want] feel?" again and again, if you must. Contemplate it. You may flip-flop between feeling good and feeling bad moment to moment, but your nervous system will prefer the good feeling, and it will take root and begin to grow. It must, because you care about how you feel, you are determined; and because you always reach for a better feeling.

I was working with a woman who wanted to feel safe. When she asked herself how safe feels, she said it felt nervous. This is an example of the slippery mind in action. She said it felt nervous, "because she had to be on guard." Trained therapists could miss this and think she needs to (mentally) discuss how being on guard has nothing to do with safe…and off we could go with the complex mind, when really this is quite simple.

The feeling she was accessing was not the feeling "safe," it was the feeling of "being on guard," which was not a good feeling. In this situation there are two options: persist in seeking what safe really feels like (it *must* feel good), or ask herself what she wanted instead of "being on guard" (perhaps being "relaxed"), and then put them together by asking, "How does feeling relaxed and safe feel?" and go forward from there.

FEELING DOES NOT HAVE DIRECTION

The moment you feel love "for" someone, or some thing, or some event, you are just feeling love. "Feeling loved" (by them) is the same thing as just feeling love. Loving someone else is the same thing as feeling love. There is only love. *And* it is only created and experienced in one place—within you.

That said, when you want to feel "someone's love," it might also include a feeling of connection with them. So, what you are seeking and calling love may have a different "flavor" at different times. When you access your partner's love it would feel different from how you experience your mother's love. You know the difference, and so that is why I will specifically ask "How does your partner's love feel?" Whatever the "flavor" of the feeling, it resides only within you, so you do not need someone's presence or particular actions in order to know and have this feeling.

YOU POWER FEELING

{ Appreciation is a wonderful thing.
It makes what is wonderful in others belong to us as well. ~ Voltaire }

You will notice that with a little attention to how someone's love feels, that as you take some time and enjoy it, it will begin to grow. Appreciating this good feeling, it will grow even more. As it grows, you can feel love for the feeling of love itself. Notice that as it expands it has no object. It is just a great loving feeling, and it is completely fulfilling. The same goes for happiness, peace, and all other emotions.

Conversely, the same mechanism exists for anger. When we were angry and initially attributed it to one event, that is how as the feeling grew we could become miserable with and angry at the whole world; in actuality, the whole of our experience. That is also how, when feeling great sadness, the whole world and everything in it can seem sad.

Of course that can't *be*—the world is not sad—it is just that in putting all of our attention on the bad feeling, we build up this great sadness, so large and thick, and we put all of our attention on it, eliminating any other possibilities, ignoring the rest of the totality of reality. If we put our whole attention on sadness, then we can't see, hear, feel, or know anything else.

During suffering there is always good feeling available as a possibility. In the same way that you are the power for thoughts, you are the power of feeling.

This ability of feeling to expand and become large and abstract, for better or worse, is illustrated next in a State of Being Scale.

Chapter 10

You can't skip what's now

People have asked, "Why can't I just not let it bother me?"

Yes, why can't you? *Because it already does.* Sometimes people don't want to answer the first *Alchemy* question, they don't want to discover what it is they want; they just want not to be bothered by whatever it is. I have seen people get intensely frustrated and angry (more suffering) trying to skip being attached, when they already are.

Yes, *ultimately* you want to be free from attachment to the outside, but that would mean attachment and its neediness and associated bad feeling does not even arise. However, if you are feeling any degree of suffering, it has already arisen. It means you are *already* attached to something and that you are denying yourself some specific feeling. There is a particular bad thought-feeling that can be used to discover and address the attachment. Otherwise the attachment and belief remain and the problem will resurface when triggered again.

After you have practiced staying here and now with body awareness and have been self-fulfilling enough to know, at least mentally, that you are *all* you will ever need, then accepting what is becomes easier and easier because you don't want or need it to be different.

After you use *Alchemy*, then deeply accept what is. That means, after shifting your state, continue keeping your attention on the feeling in the body and recognize with complete, absolute, and utter acceptance mentally, emotionally, energetically, and physically what is, *perfectly as it is, now*. Accept what is the way you relax into and accept the heat from a hot bath. Invite it to penetrate. If your positive energy drops, or you notice a desire to resist or change what is, then start over with *Alchemy* and repeat looking at and accepting what is. It will get easier and easier, and you will come to see and know the positive value of what is. Continue considering all the ways how "what is" is good.

Each adverse situation gives you an excellent opportunity to face adversity feeling good and to accept what is, now. So you can use *Alchemy* for presence, and vice versa.

There could be a number of motivations for a desire to skip the issue that bothers you (the attachment): you may not want to face what the issue is, you may be impatient, or you may be highly motivated to be detached from the outside. In any case, attempting to skip is akin to denying what is, so it will not work.

Wanting to be "stronger" than it is will also not work as that implies resistance, and what you resist persists because your attention is still on it. The stronger your effort, the more your attention is on it, the stronger *it* will get. *You* don't need to be stronger than *your* attachment—an impossibility anyway, because you are it.

Your strength does not come from being bigger or better or stronger; it comes from realizing there is no thing to fight. It comes from seeing that you already felt good before you decided to feel bad. The only strength you need is a strong desire to *feel good*.

Some people object that they don't want to give themselves what they want, they don't want to "give in" to their desire. This is not being weak or "giving in" to your desire because we are not talking about changing the outside circumstance that you are attached to. You are not going to get the thing, person, or event; you are going to detach from needing them.

We are talking about having the strength to be utterly honest with yourself about what it is that you in truth *do* want (even if you have judged that to be petty or selfish). If you need any strength, you need it to use the mirror of the outside world to look within and discover your attachment so you can use *Alchemy* to release it.

The attachment's mirror, or opposite feeling, will quench it. To know what is missing, we need to look *at* the mirror, not away from it. The first question, "What do you want?" uses the outside (which you think you need) to get to the missing feeling inside.

To detach, give yourself what you want *without getting it from the outside.* That is how you will learn, again and again, that no thing and no one outside of you can hurt you. Eventually, you will notice opportunities to suffer arise, and you will not take the bait, because you know you have another, better feeling option and you will no longer have a "reason" to suffer. The wind will be knocked out of the sail of suffering.

If you just want to "feel better"—in spite of a situation—and to just gloss over things, then you could also be avoiding looking at the truth, the egoic habits, which when seen will be known as how small and petty they really are, but seeing them will enable you to drop them. There is nothing to fear in looking at them, and everything (ongoing suffering) to fear in not looking at them.

If you try to gloss over it and do not look deeply enough to make this discovery, then even if you are able to know a better feeling in the moment, the attachment will still be intact and so the problem will resurface, again and again.

Using *Alchemy* allows expansion to know your infinite self and to feel good doing it, which only makes sense. Whereas moving away from the grandeur of who you truly are is painful.

If you still cling to wanting to "not be affected" by something, what will that give you? First of all, not wanting to be bothered by "it" still implies and believes that *it* can *do* something *to* you; that it actually has some power (which it does not). As well, wanting to "not be affected by it" is a negative and you can't give yourself a negative. What would that be?

If you were to state what you want in the positive, what would that be? It could be many things: "peace" perhaps? Say a situation "made" you feel judged. So as you are already feeling judged, try just giving yourself peace. You can see how it won't work. While you are feeling judged you cannot feel peaceful. As well, trying to force something else, something a different size, shape, or quality into that void will not work either.

The perceived problem outside is only a mirror for what is missing inside, so what you *do* want will be the opposite of what you don't want. When you are feeling judged, for example, you might be *wanting* acceptance. Until you give yourself acceptance, you will feel judged—and you can't know peace. When you give yourself what you want and change your state, then you are free and cannot fall for the false appearance of being affected by the outside.

The "Gleb State of Being Scale" was born while chatting with a reader who drew me to delve deeply into the process of changing state. Later I was led to enhance the scale by other readers I met who just wanted to skip their issue and feel better.

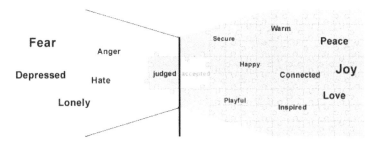

Bad feeling ⟵---------------------------------------⟶ Good feeling

Strong – Abstract – Contraction   Strong – Abstract – Expansion

Notice the mirror, how the missing piece is the opposite feeling; e.g., feeling judged is really not feeling acceptance. Also notice that the further away you get from something specific, like judged, and the closer you get to abstract thoughts and generalizations (toward the left), the harder you contract and the worse it feels, like depression.

THE STRUCTURE OF DEPRESSIVE THINKING

When we generalize, words can become "frozen" in time, in a form of language called a "nominalization." The word "depression" is a nominalization. There is no movement or action in this word. It is *perceived* as a *real* thing, a static, non-changing, abstract, conceptual thing. It's much harder to do something about "a depression," than to do something about how you are "depressing" yourself. Doing something that is depressing you is doing something specific, it is in action, it is moving, and it can change.

The word "depression" appears so solid that it can seem almost like a concrete, unchanging "thing"—one that you must now fight "against." But it's just a word! It is a concept; a flimsy thought that like all thoughts, comes and goes, unless *you* hold it.

Any word that ends in "ion" is a nominalization that is stuck. The way to deal with one is to turn it into a verb. For example, to respond to the generalization, "There's no communication here!" a useful response would be to ask, "How would you like to be communicating?" Now that's something we can do something about.

You can generalize, delete, distort and "nominalize" yourself into a horrible state that doctors would label "depression." In an effort to "grasp" them and to know how to universally deal with a complex, eternally changing organism, the medical profession likes labeling as frozen things which are actually processes.

Unwittingly, labeling processes (verbs) as things (nouns) makes them mentally more difficult to deal with for both the doctor and the patient. A diagnosis is a nominalization and also a belief. How little power is there in that? In truth, every "dis-ease" is a process, and known and viewed as such, it is constantly changing, and therefore changeable.

Perhaps when mental suffering and depressing is severe enough or goes on long enough, it alters the brain chemistry, which makes it more difficult to naturally correct, and the patient may need to turn to medication, hopefully temporarily, until the body-mind can resume healthy functioning.

In the reverse of this, and on the flip side of the scale, good feeling can also become generalized and abstract, and grow into strong, expansive experiences at the other end, with love, peace, and joy.

THOUGHT DELETIONS, DISTORTIONS, AND GENERALIZATIONS

Every human experience, even the most simple one, is vast. Each moment includes infinite sights, sounds, tastes, touches, thoughts, and feelings and various flavors of each. Each and every living moment, your body-mind is simultaneously sensing and knowing all of this, and you store it (as best you can) as memory.

When you attempt to communicate your past experience, you can't just "download" your full knowing, your full experience, to someone else. You have to use words; words that are not the experience itself, but which are an attempt to convey the experience and any conclusion about the experience (i.e., what you decided it meant to you).

So words have to take the place of the experience, and in that they are a poor substitute at best. Unless you want to sit talking and detailing for hours, you eliminate much about the experience (deletion), and you group, or generalize, other things. The fewer words you use, the more you have lost in the sharing. Even if you do sit talking for hours, *words are still not the experience* and much is always lost, regardless.

As well, memory is not carved in stone; it is "plastic," so every time you recall and tell a story of the past, you "re-store" it as a new memory, a slightly altered experience, which now includes any new perceptions, insights, beliefs, or conclusions you've acquired since. This is why and how time "changes" things, for better or worse. Of course, what happened has not changed, but your perception, understanding, memory, or acceptance of it changes. This is how in coaching sessions we can "change" the past. In reality what is changed is your present recall and perception of the past—in the now.

That ability to alter memory is continually available and continually running, and without conscious discretion, it is under the dictatorship of mind-reads, powered by your fears and attachments. On its own, it can delete, distort, and generalize your memory of what actually happened into a new, quite different, limiting, and even extremely painful "memory" now.

Have you ever played the childhood game where kids sit in a circle and a secret sentence is whispered from ear to ear? If you have not played this as a kid, I highly recommend you do it now as an adult.

The sentence may start as, "The white dog ran through the puddle," but by the time it reaches the last person, it can become, "The hog is a big fat farm animal," or something even quite unintelligent and incoherent. The more ears it is whispered through, the crazier it gets. This is an entertaining social game, however more importantly it is also a powerful lesson in thought-feeling.

The more you "talk to yourself" or others in a painful way about something, the more deleting, distorting, and generalizing you can do, and the uglier and more unintelligent what you are saying can become.

Suffering can begin with a very specific and benign circumstance or event, followed by a painful thought about it. If that thought and pain are believed as your entire truth and reality, if thoughts about the pain continue, and if something or someone outside is made the "evil cause" and blamed as the "why," then the line of thinking will deteriorate to include deletions, distortions, or generalizations, and the suffering will grow in intensity.

Here's an example: your boss tells you that you made an error on the records. In your mind that may become, "He thinks I am a screw-up" (mind-read), "He judged me" (distortion), "How dare he!" (anger), "He always does this" (generalization), "I can't do anything right" (deletion, generalization), "I'm going to lose my job (distortion) and become depressed just like always" (deletion, distortion, generalization).

But none of that is real or true now; it's all just a bad unconscious dream. Your boss simply said you made an error. Reality, or truth, is always much kinder than the thoughts we have tended to think and believe *about* it. That very action itself, superimposing a thought on reality, which seems defensive, creates separation, and is actually *offensive*. It is completely unnecessary, and certainly not useful.

The higher "stacked" and more distorted thought-feelings become, and the more generalized or abstract they become, the more painful they become, and the harder they can be to untangle or manage. Then it becomes all about the pain and, as the ultimate generalization, you can become convinced that your thoughts are true and real *simply because it hurts so much.*

However, the reason those thoughts hurt so much is because they are *not* true. It hurts so much because you have contracted yourself so hard into an experience of negative thinking that is not the reality of what the experience was—and not who you inherently are.

So memory and thoughts about the past, used as a reason to suffer, are poor witnesses. Of course, no matter how good the testimony of this witness is, you don't have to believe any of it now. The past can only hurt in the present. So then, is it the past?

FREEDOM

You may be highly motivated for freedom, but if you are suffering, then you are still feeling and experiencing attachment. Go inside and give yourself what is missing so you can detach and erode the old belief that has kept you tethered to the ever-changing, uncontrollable, unreliable outside. You can get personal insights around the issue, and you may also get insights that have to do with non-separation.

How often you will use suffering to point you toward joy is up to you. Committing to not blaming the outside, committing to going inside and consciously choosing what you are truly most interested in (a better feeling, right?) combined with your power of attention will bring relief fast.

Wanting to skip the issue you are attached to is not all bad, it also means you are aware in the moment because you know suffering is present and you don't want to have that as your experience. You are witnessing, you have separated yourself from the suffering, and now have an opportunity. If you face the perceived "bad" thing with it's antidote, the experience you desire, you will gain insights, and perhaps even the final insight: how free and powerful you really are.

Yes, ultimately we want to be free from all attachment to the outside and, therefore at peace, but until you consciously experience your innate freedom free as your reality, as truth, you will not know it without doubt, and attachment will continue to arise.

To know in the truth of your experience that you are free from the outside, to know experientially the source of feeling, you need to experience it (feeling) *as* yourself, which is the opposite of what you have believed you have experienced and known.

Practice giving yourself everything you were specifically denying yourself—in the face of the perceived adversity. Clearly observe and acknowledge the existence of both the apparent adverse circumstances and your freedom of good feeling, as separate yet simultaneous. Each specific suffering situation gives you a shot at knowing truth as you experience reality through a new way of being.

SIMPLIFY, SIMPLIFY, SIMPLIFY

Happiness is simple, but people have become so complicated through living complex, conceptual, limiting thoughts and beliefs that we must clean the slate. Simply notice how you feel, and become comfortable with not knowing other people's meaning or purpose, because uncertainty is the only place that possibilities lie.

Drop everything you thought you knew and return to the childlike purity of not knowing. But don't worry; it's only that which causes you pain that you are going to lose and "unlearn."

CHAPTER 11

The Insights

We have confused things, people, and events for feeling. *No thing, person, or event can make you feel.* No thing, person, or event can hurt you. No thing contains your joy. Take for example, a new car. Where, actually, is the joy within two tons of metal? If you did not have a good feeling, how much less would you care about the car? It just becomes the practical (or impractical) thing it already is.

You can associate things, people, and events with feeling, and live as if you have no other choice, but that is a formula for suffering. Usually this association is unconscious; we are not aware of it, and so we mistake what we want: the feeling (inside), for the person, event or thing "out there." Then because "out there" often does not cooperate with us, we suffer. Mistaking ourselves to be this small, powerless being, we pretend to give our power away, although that can never be real or true.

When you recognize that it was you who set the "rules" about when you can feel joy and when you must suffer, not only can you change the rules—you can decide to ditch the rules. When you ditch the rules you abandon attachment to the outside, and only then can you discover the "treasure house" within.

{ Your treasure house is within, it contains all you'll ever need.

~ Hui Hai }

{ While you go looking for trinkets,
your treasure house awaits you in your own being. ~ Rumi }

{ For indeed, the kingdom of God is within you.
~ Jesus, Luke 17:20–21 }

{ This satisfaction born within isn't equaled by ordinary treasure.
~ Milarepa }

DON'T LOOK FOR REASONS FOR YOUR PAIN

One of the most important understandings that has come to me is that pain is not telling you to go outside and look for the "reason" for it, or to seek the "cause" of it, outside you. That "reason" will support and sustain your "reality," "need," or "right" to suffer, and that will only support your belief that something outside of you can make you feel bad or good. It is the reason we give for suffering that *creates* the suffering, and that reason will keep you bound, tethered to, and at the mercy of the uncontrollable winds of change, again and again.

When you go looking for reasons for your pain, you will "find" them (or perceive them as such). That will be *so easy* to do because when you feel bad, bad thoughts come to you easily and effortlessly, and what you are actually doing is looking for something to "fit" as a cause, and by doing so, you will actually *create* a reason, or multiple reasons! What you seek to know, you will know. That may not be our intention, still it is the fruit of our actions.

Why did we look for reasons? Perhaps because we thought the outside was the cause and therefore thought that changing it was necessary in order to feel better. You may not be able to change the outside as desired, and as long as you try to with attachment, you will suffer. If you do succeed, then the relief will only be temporary, until the outside changes again. In addition, the relief will be incomplete, not true relief, final and complete—not true satisfaction, freedom, and peace.

Think of a recent time when you didn't feel good, when you had a sense of a problem. Take your time to find one. OK, have one? Now consider this question: If you did not feel bad, would there be a problem? Most will answer no, and agree that there may still be things to do, but there is no sense of problem. It's not necessary to change the outside in order to feel okay, in order to feel good inside. Something outside of you is not the feeling inside.

{ The best things in life aren't things. - Art Buchwald }

SEEK JOY! ...THE ONLY PLACE IT CAN BE FOUND. INSIDE.

Give up attachment to needing anything outside in order to feel good. This does not mean you do not take action or make changes. It means you do it feeling good.

Whatever attention is on, you experience. With your attention on reasons, then attention is on the problem and the suffering. You will never find what you *do* want looking at what you don't want. It's just not there. This is why it is critical when answering the second *Alchemy* question "How does it feel?" to answer it in the positive, and to keep your attention on how it *does* feel (not on how it doesn't feel).

WE HAVE BECOME GOOD AT SUFFERING

When you were crying as a child and your parents did not want to listen to you, what did they do? If they were like my parents, they said, "If you want to cry, go to your room!" and you went to your room. What for? As commanded, to cry, right? Perhaps you cried even more, or even harder.

How often were you sent to your room to feel good? Right, never. So we became really good at suffering. (Suggestion to parents: come up with something else, anything else. Please, let's break this pattern.)

We have been conditioned to use the noticing of a bad feeling as a cue to go be unhappy. As an adult your habit may still be to go to the bedroom and cry, or to go for a walk and stew over it. But suffering is pointing you toward joy. So now, when you feel bad, I am sending you to your room—to *feel good!*

Whether you take a walk or go to your bedroom, do it with your sole interest in feeling better. Go have a Feel Good Fest! Ask yourself what you want, and begin to feel it. Notice the smile that grows and enjoy that. Allow the good feeling to grow into love, joy, or peace. If you are in bed, snuggle into the sheets and pillows, enjoying that. You may even relax so much that you fall into a rejuvenating nap.

Nothing is Bad

There is an ancient story that illustrates that nothing is bad; it's about a farmer whose horse ran away. When his neighbors heard the news, they went to see him.

"What terrible luck," they said.

The farmer responded with, "We'll see."

The next morning the horse returned, bringing with it three other wild horses.

"This is great news," his neighbors said excitedly.

"We'll see," repeated the old man.

The following day, his son tried to tame one of the wild horses, was thrown off, and broke his leg.

Once again, the neighbors offered their sympathy.

"We'll see," said the farmer.

The next day the army came through, drafting young men to fight for the emperor.

The son couldn't serve because of his broken leg. The neighbors congratulated the farmer on his good luck.

"We'll see" said the farmer.

Good and bad mentally divide up that which cannot be divided, that which does not end. This story illustrates how everything changes, and how nothing is separate from what comes next. By labeling things as good or bad we attempt to isolate and separate, but this can only be done mentally, not actually. I have come to know that nothing is bad, because it is also good, and because it cannot be separated that way.

"All-or-none thinking" is one of the cognitive errors often corrected in therapy, yet the whole of our society has all-or-none thinking, with the core belief that something is either good or bad.

In my life, from abuse, to being judged and abandoned, to the "badness" of my father's death, they all resulted in something good, although beliefs can blind one to that.

As well, "good" or "bad" are thought-feelings. Events are not feeling. These two are not the same thing, and they both just exist, they just are. But a bad thought-feeling, believed in, can blind you to truth.

Events, things, or people are not inherently good or bad; our thinking-feeling good or bad is. Every thing that is, is. Resistance to what is, is suffering. When you love what "is," every thing is good. Living, seeing, being this way, there is finally peace and joy of Being, no matter what.

I distinctly remember my first conscious injury as a child. As I stared at the wound and noticed the previously unknown experience; the simultaneous moving, tingling, and burning for which I had no words, I called for Mom. Pointing at it, I tried to describe the sensations with words I knew and with curiosity, I asked,

"*What is that?*"

She said "It's pain."

"Oh." I said.

To which she added, "It's *bad.*"

"Ohhhh, then…*stop it!*" I yelled as I thrust my hand up at her. Before I was told it was bad, it was just new, unknown sensations, unjudged. It just was. Pain, I did not know. *Bad,* I did.

{ There is nothing either good or bad, but thinking makes it so.

~ Shakespeare }

Even knowing a "bad" feeling moving within you is not bad. What can it do? You can just notice it, without indulgence or repression. Notice that the only constant is change, and that a bad feeling will change when you don't give it a "dwelling place" by thinking it is real and solid.

Nothing is inherently bad or good, you don't need a reason to be happy, and even with a "reason" to be unhappy, you can be happy!

SUFFERING MEANS IT IS TIME TO FEEL GOOD—NOTHING ELSE

When you are feeling bad, you cannot simultaneously feel good. It's really that simple. Internal pain is an indicator that you are not feeling whole, that you are not internally experiencing what you prefer. Feeling bad does not mean it is time to look for an outside reason or cause—it means it's time to give yourself what you want, inside.

Now when a "negative" feeling does begin to arise in my experience, the rare gift of it does not last long because it is simply a pointer to freedom and joy, which I gratefully accept.

That feels so vastly better that I no longer believe in my "self."

CHAPTER 12

The False Relief of "self"

Saying I loved someone more than my "self" sounds strangely funny to me now, because I have absolutely no affection for the separated self that I thought existed. Now I recognize the idea of a separate self, of separation is *the source* of all suffering.

Back then it was a serious struggle. The only previously known ways of making oneself feel better after a bad experience—those "separation" strategies which we have been handed down out of ignorance—were strongly ingrained habits that replayed repeatedly: "He's an idiot," "She is not compassionate," "She has an attitude," "He always ignores me," "She did not love me," "He plays favorites," etc. These old strategies can be used to prop up and stroke the self* by putting down the other*; to find a way to blame, or a belief so that we would be justified, defended, or released.

But it's never complete, is it? Some bad taste remains because: (1) blame is a negative thought-feeling, and (2) you have created "self and other"—"separation"—which is in itself painful, and (3) you have not resolved the perceived issue inside that enables you to experience a problem "outside." So the pattern will repeat with someone else until you know and practice the other option, the joy of non-separation.

The moment there is a self, there automatically is an "other." So now there is a "you" separate from "me." The very existence of the idea of self and other creates the illusion of separation, and with that comes all manner of suffering. Then "you" and "me" develop self-ish interests that can come into conflict.

Separated, we also experience being very tiny and small against the rest of the world—but the rest of the world is not against you; every moment it is here, *supporting your very existence*.

Without it, there *is* no you.

> { When the I, the Me, and the Mine are dead,
>   the work of the Lord is done. } ~ Kabir

Looking deeper we will see that scientists and sages alike agree: there is no separation.

CHAPTER 13

There Is No Separation

When I hear people speak of connection in a painful way, I know that there is a fundamental belief in separation because where there is no separation, there is no need for connection. In order to believe in connection you must believe in separation—but both connection and separation are conceptual.

There are many ways separation can be obviously exposed as fundamentally false, and without separation, connection is redundant.

At most, these are both actually forms of feeling; you feel separate or you feel connected. Do you sense when someone is upset? Even in a crowd of strangers, the predominant group energy is felt and in that way could seem "transmitted." We've seen how panic can spread instantly in crowds and how synchronized rocking to beautiful songs can happens in crowds. Whatever you are feeling you are also offering to others. It manifests in your presence, body language, voice, words, and in your actions.

Instead of looking at all the ways in which we appear separate, we can look at some obvious ways that separation is a myth. If you look at the reality of your experience, the food in your bowl that you eat becomes your body, the air you breathe in and out is the same air billions of people and trees breathe in and out. Then there is the way you define yourself in comparison and contrast (or opposition) to others and apart from everything else, there *is* no you.

Within the seamless whole, there appears to be differentiation—for without it there would be no experience—but there is no separation. Those are some ways in which we are not separate.

As well, scientists now know that there is "no thing" out there *to be* separate; that at the smallest level, everything is energy, vibration, movement, and so there is no separate, concrete thing, and that includes our bodies.

{ The atoms or elementary particles themselves are not real;
they form a world of potentialities or possibilities
rather than one of things or facts.
~ Werner Heisenberg, Physics Nobel Prize recipient, 1932 }

{ Everything we call real is made of things
that cannot be regarded as real.
~ Niels Bohr, Physics Nobel Prize recipient, 1922 }

{ Observations not only disturb what is to be measured,
they produce it. ~ Pascual Jordan, physicist }

{ What a shift! In a radically different interpretation of
our relationship to the world, Wheeler is stating that it's impossible
for us to simply watch the world happen around us. We can never
be observers, because when we observe, we create and modify what
is created….the discoveries of the last century suggest that our act
of observing the world is an act of creation unto itself. And it's consciousness that is doing the creating! These findings seem to support
Wheeler's proposition that we can no longer consider ourselves merely
as onlookers who have no effect on the world that we're observing.
~ Gregg Braden, *The Spontaneous Healing of Belief* }

{ Like a wave I rise in my body,
sea and wave the same wild water. ~ Rumi }

When you literally come to your senses, it becomes very obvious that there is no separation. Sound is one sense that we can use. Playing with the nature of experience with a friend as we watched a plane cross the sky, I asked, "Where is the sound?"

"In the airplane," she said.

"So, without the air, is there sound?" I asked again.

"Hmmm noooo…" was the contemplative reply she gave before adding, "It's in the airwaves."

"So then, without the eardrum, is there sound?"

Now she looked at me with a bit of frustration mixed with confusion. Sound is an excellent experience to explore reality with. One could say that it is experienced "in here" in the brain, yet, without the airplane, would there be sound? You see, it is a trick question, and one that we fall for only because we believe in separation.

In the question itself there is an assumption—that there is a "where" the sound is. We believe there is a "where" because we believe there is a here that is separate from it. And so the question itself is never questioned; we just attempt to answer it. But sound is not divided up into "here" and "there."

That's just a thought, an idea which, under the scrutiny of reality, cannot hold up. In the same way, I have found that with close observation, no experience can be divided up and separated—including sight, touch, or taste. You cannot separate yourself from any of it. Indeed, if you were *truly* separate, you could not experience any of it.

The idea of separation is a trick of mind, although a powerful one because everything in your experience points to non-separation, yet *still* we are able to turn our heads from the obvious and imagine we are separate. We have built our whole life and experience around this idea. Non-separation is more than an idea or concept, and if deeply recognized, its fact changes your whole experience of life in a fundamental way.

Even as you walk across your house from one room to another, feeling the floor change beneath your feet, you are still only here. There is only here and now, and the experience of now is always changing, perhaps from the feel of the kitchen hardwood to the living room shag.

When you begin to experience the undivided reality as it is, and stop taking the stance and perspective that you are here and everything else is there, then the world begins to seem a little less big and scary—or is it that you seem a little larger…?

Question the unspoken assumptions and concepts about your experience that you were taught since you were a child. After all, they are the foundation for everything else you believe in life! Paying attention to your actual life, and not your concepts and ideas—not to *thoughts about* your life—you can use the powerful experience of your direct senses to challenge and loosen the idea of separation.

Practice non-separation

The senses are undeniable and are always directly here, available to bring you back to now; however, the fleeting, insubstantial, imaginary thoughts that we can use to separate ourselves from others and reality can have no limits. Because we've had a lifetime of creating and practicing them, there are hundreds, maybe thousands of ways to blame and separate!

And because we've had a lifetime of convincing ourselves, sharing, agreeing on, and gossiping with blame and separation, the habit of so doing may be strong. The belief in the "relief" of it may be strong. But, that relief is never complete and pure, is it?—and it's never permanent. So no matter what comes up, refuse to accept the thought, and certainly do not act on it. Neither you, yourself, nor any other person is any one thought.

WE ARE ALL MUCH MORE THAN A THOUGHT

Holding a separating belief about someone and defending it with, "but it's *true*, I *know* him," is one way we can do violence to others. How vain. Who am I to define someone for life? Who am I to condemn them to limitation? When we "box" and limit someone, we also limit ourselves. We limit our experience of them, and we limit our relationship with them. What value is there in repeatedly thinking limiting or negative thoughts about others?

Even when I hear someone else define and limit themselves, I do not buy into it, I do not support it, I do not repeat it, I do not hold space for it, I do not keep it in my reality, and I do not project it into theirs. Even if they repeat a limit for years. Have you ever known people to change? People change all the time, consciously or unconsciously. To change consciously all you have to do is hear and change what you have been repeating to yourself and others. That will make space for other possibilities, because when nothing is certain, everything is possible.

When I hear a self-proclaimed belief of any sort, I hold in mind that the person is having a temporary bad dream and that they are much bigger than any one thought held in the moment.

You can prove this for yourself. Write down a limiting belief about yourself in this format: "I am _____." For example: "I am a sad person."

Then take some time to ask and answer each of the following questions[1] fully. Sometimes you may get a verbal answer with a feeling. Other times maybe just the sense of a shift.

Pause after each, contemplating and staying with each question until nothing else comes. You can even write it here:

"I am _____."

([1]This is an NLP exercise by John Overdurf)

Ready?

"Is that *ALL* that you think you are?"

"You're much more than that, aren't you?"

"What are you that's NOT that?"

"And how much more are you than all of *that*?"

"How do you know?"

~

Do you notice that these thoughts feel better? Which do you prefer? How much more did you come up with than the first little original thought? So now you see, no matter what you think you are, you are *always* more than that. You *have* to be. And so are others!

Every label is a limit. A thought is a tiny, fleeting phenomenon, and whether it's about yourself or someone else, if it does not serve connection, if it does not serve your highest purpose and largest sense of self, if it does not *feel* good, then let it go by seeking joy, by picking up something that feels better, something that does serve. *Seek joy!*

The only belief—if any—that I hold about myself or others is that we are unlimited.

No thought, no sentence, is who you are, nor can one limit you. This brings us back to revisit concepts again, but this time perhaps one of the most "sticky" types of concept, spiritual concepts.

We've been parroting concepts and false beliefs so long that in some cases it's become an unconscious habit. They have even been dressed up in the guise of many "spiritual" concepts, and who dare argue with those? Yet these may be the worst kind, because we can be so righteous with them, and they seem "good," so how can they be wrong? But the best intention in the world will not make the false true. Even well-intentioned concepts can be roadblocks, and in fact they can be major sticking points *because* they appear and feel good.

Concepts are simply concepts, and like other thoughts they can be a tool. At one time, they may have served you well. They may have brought you to where you are now, but like boats that take you across rivers, in order to continue on your journey, you must at some point abandon them. To find truth, you must raise the bar and reject what is simply conceptual for you. A concept will never truly, ultimately satisfy you; it will always create and leave more questions.

When you love truth, you will drop empty, unreal concepts; and when others speak them, you will notice them as such. Now they jump out and glare at me. Like the common spiritual one of speaking about, "My higher self." That implies a second "lower self," –and a third self that knows both of these? Are there *three* of you? How about these three come forward and show themselves all at once?

Sages have said things that are not concepts *to them*, but which are alive in and *as* them, like "We are one." However, mind can say

"Ohhhh, I like that," and grab the idea repeat it, and teach it—of course only *as a thought*—and without the authority of direct *Knowing*, it can proclaim "We are one."

Satisfied?

I hope not. I hope you become curious beyond concepts, because you may believe, "We are one"—but perhaps only until your neighbor leaves rotting garbage locked in their garage while on vacation for four months, and then you are one with everyone but him. Parroted concepts can make you a hypocrite.

{ What you don't see with your eyes, don't invent with your mouth.
~ Yiddish proverb }

{ Embody what you teach, and teach only what you have embodied.
~ Socrates character in the book, *The Way of the Peaceful Warrior* }

It does not matter what religion you follow, if any. When a truth is embodied, there is no effort involved in trying to be a certain way. Trying to be good will not make you into a Jesus or a Buddha. It is good to hold good values, but in the effort you will not be perfect at all times, so don't be hard on yourself.

It is not because they act in a wholesome manner that they are Jesus and Buddha; they act in a wholesome manner because they are Jesus and Buddha. Right thought, speech, and action do not arise from them because they are trying to be good, it does not happen through effort. When you know others and the seamless, undivided whole to be your very self, you cannot act otherwise.

Wholesome action arises spontaneously *as a result* of clear seeing. You don't need to "become" a Jesus or Buddha, you need to see what they see.

*{ Trying to follow in the footsteps
of the masters,*
but it's a lot harder than it looks
because even though they had
the same size feet as us,
they weren't looking down the whole time
while they walked to make sure
they were doing it right.
~ Brian Andreas }

The whole spiritual movement is erroneously thought to be a journey of "becoming," a growing and improving of your self. Perhaps that inclination is rooted in religious beliefs of being born imperfect, or the material, capitalistic world where things are improved and business is grown. However, you don't need to "become" a better person, awakening is not about becoming.

Like the Buddha or Jesus, you just need to see or know who you really are (and who you are not). Any value in the spiritual movement is the inner drive for that truth, and nothing short of seeing of that truth (no knowledge, no learning, no growth) can set you free. In fact, knowledge, especially ideas of who you are and how you are growing, stands in the way.

Such mere thought knowledge and belief leave no room for truth (or reality). A belief is just absence of doubt. In the absence of doubt, we stagnate. Then we live out of our head, out of what we think we already know.

This living out of your head in thought to the exclusion of experience literally affects even your direct senses. On my blog you will find an article about meeting a man and sensing something was "wrong" with him, but not being able to know what exactly it was. After three disturbed visits during which time it seemed I could not really see him as more than a blur, it took asking myself questions, one-by-one, about him until I discovered what it was. With doubt for what I knew, I asked myself the color of his clothes, and the color of his hair, and the color of his eyes, and that was when I clearly looked at each eye separately and was finally able to see that one was blue—and one was grey! Suddenly, I could see his eyes, and *I could clearly see him*! (That experience was very similar to the sudden, clear, direct seeing of Self that I experienced in the woods, recounted in the Prologue).

In that moment I realized, it is not the eyes that see, but the mind. When we live out of thought, or what we already believe we "know," we are severely limited.

Scientists have proven this. There was an experiment with kittens that were raised from birth in a cage with vertical white and black stripes, who later could not see horizontal lines and fell over table tops and stairs. It makes you wonder what potentially all of us are not seeing.

When we have been conditioned, do not pay attention to what's actually going on, have not taken time to question beliefs, or if we are not comfortable with not knowing, the mind wants to take the easy, quick way out by grabbing a readily available concept or something previously known. But it's actually not the easy way because you hurt while believing painful concepts and you can be blocked by good or spiritual concepts.

Even though concepts are not good enough, you may not want to let go of concepts before having knowing, however you will only have knowing after you let go of concepts, because there is no room for knowing anything else.

There is an ancient Zen story that illustrates this. A seeker visited a Zen master to learn about Zen and tea was made ready. As the master spoke the seeker kept interrupting, telling the master about all he knew. Finally the master stopped talking and began to serve the tea, but he kept pouring until the cup overflowed. The seeker jumped up and said "Enough! Stop, no more can go into the cup."

"Exactly, said the master, like this cup you are full of your own concepts and speculations. How can I show you Zen if you do not empty your cup?"

~

It's not just negative concepts and thoughts that can fortify a sense of separate self, or "ego"—anything we use to prop-up the self, including spiritual concepts, can be a roadblock. Drop them, and you will notice (1) that you keep breathing and then (2) that other previously hidden possibilities will become obvious.

NON-SEPARATION, THEREFORE NON-EGO

Yet, I have returned full circle to know that ego does not exist. Ego was simply a collection of habitual thoughts or feelings about you. Of course, none of them can *be* you.

It was your own, voluntary, conceptual separation from all that you truly are, from all that has always been and always is available to you now, that caused pain.

It was an idea of something missing, a sense of lack, a wanting, an idea of separation from something or everything—from all that *can't be separate*. Therefore, there is nothing, no ego, to subdue; there is only the all-encompassing joy of Being to embrace.

COMPASSION

Compassion is not feeling someone else's pain. Compassion is knowing that suffering is universal, and a wish that another person not suffer. You can't feel someone else's suffering. You don't have their body or mind, and you identify with yours. You may be aware that someone is suffering, but if you believe you are feeling their suffering, you are feeling your own body-mind and your own suffering, based on a belief that someone should not suffer. Your suffering for this reason and in this way has a different flavor and is a different experience from their suffering. It is based on the belief that if someone suffers, that you must also suffer.

This is falsely founded on the belief that your suffering will help the other. But if you turn to someone who is suffering with pain and suffering on *your* face and in *your* voice, as you say, "Ohhh, that must hurt *so* much," you may well trigger *more* suffering in them. Worse yet, you can feed attachment and the feeble egoic sense of self by making them feel justified in their suffering. Like blame, this kind of affirmation may help someone feel a tiny bit better, but like blaming, it is never pure, never complete, and leaves a bad taste.

You don't have to suffer to show you care, and it is a poor way to try to help them. The blind cannot lead the blind; you can't be poor enough to help the poor (one of the best things you can do for the poor is to not be one of them), and you cannot help someone's suffering with your own suffering. To help, to give, you must *have*.

THE BEST WAY TO END SOMEONE ELSE'S SUFFERING
IS TO END YOUR OWN

Be in a better place so you can hold space for it, show them by example, point to it; be there when they are ready to feel better, with selfless love built on the foundation of self-fulfillment. Only in that way can you, with love, truly allow them to be as they are and to be as they will become.

Cultivating compassion is a form of practicing non-separation: knowing that we are all the same and can suffer the same, your wish would be that no beings suffer. That would be all beings—including people you attempt separation from through disliking. A very interesting experiment I did was to notice when mind "pulled back" from someone it disliked, in particular strangers, and I used the noticing of that bad feeling to keep my attention on them, watching, waiting, looking for what I liked about them instead.

It did not take long until I began to see those things, and I was amazed and surprised when a feeling of love began to bubble up. Soon, love began to well up for any little reason, and no reason, everywhere, for everyone.

Believing we are a separate self, we create other, which creates conflict, destroys compassion, and creates suffering for both—and as we will see, suffering blinds you to truth.

CHAPTER 14

When We Suffer, We Can't Know Truth

"What you fear appears," is a powerful truth. I have seen someone I love suffer over something they believed about me, which could not be more *false*. It was, in fact, in complete opposition to reality. At the peak of their suffering, even when provided with the truth and evidence against their belief, they still could not stop suffering. At first my old self-centric habit was to react with hurt and pain at the false judgments. However, this gift was a wide-eye-opener, a direct viewing into the nature of delusion and suffering.

SOMEONE ELSE'S SUFFERING IS NEVER ABOUT YOU;
BECOME CURIOUS INSTEAD OF DEFENSIVE

There was such obvious lack of congruency with reality, that it just did not make any sense, and that shock helped me to drop the self and my own suffering, and to become curious instead of defensive. I saw the extreme suffering that delusion caused in that person, who in their pain was unable to receive the truth that (I thought) could ease the suffering.

I thought, "If you only knew the truth, it would all be okay." I thought truth was the answer, but I was astounded when it became apparent that while you are in a state of suffering, *truth can't be known, even if it is glaring at you*. I could do nothing; no matter how much I longed to give relief, I could not help. There was nothing I could do but watch love be destroyed through extreme delusion and suffering.

{ Every wrongful act is actually a 'cry for help' by someone deeply lost in the illusion. ~ *A Course in Miracles* }

Seeing this cracked open my heart of compassion, and is a large reason for my new work today. I have seen the delusion that suffering causes, and the suffering that delusion causes. When we suffer, all we see, hear, or feel is the pain. Nothing else. That *is* what suffering *is*. While in pain we cannot separately or objectively view what we believe is causing the pain in order to see clearly whether the perception or conclusion is even true. We cannot see everything else we know about someone, or all the other facts about the situation, *nor even our love for someone.*

Unable to see our love or their love, all kinds of untruths can be imagined and perceived as true. Yes, we can suffer over what is not true. In fact, that is mostly what we suffer over. Most of the time, our suffering is about our fears, and not about what is. Of course, even if it is "true," even if it is "what is," we still do not have to suffer. So there are layers and depths of suffering.

Not only your mind, but your awareness of your body and senses shut down during suffering. Just like when feeling hurt, abandoned or judged, feeling anger also diminishes us, our experience, our access to information, our clarity, and our intelligence. The term "blind rage" is exact; you are literally blind when angry.

I have seen such a severe state of this form of suffering that the person did not even realize that they were staring piercingly, menacingly. In this state, it seemed they did not have other behavioral options available. Suffering in any form cuts off access to your resourcefulness in every way.

The body has continual access to direct intelligence, truth. Even if held hostage and cramped with believed stressful thinking, it remains present, here and now.

It does not want to suffer and it will let you know through discomfort and pain when it is, if you pay attention to how it feels. It will let you know when you are off track so that you can become open to intelligence and clearly see what is and what is not.

MIRROR, MIRROR

While attached to the outside, the whole of apparent experience outside is a mirror of your inside. So you do not see the outside, you see only your inside. You can use this mirror to realize freedom.

We live within vast richness, with variety and multiple options. This life presents opportunity for preference, for choice. I had an experience with someone where I was noting the contrast between print qualities of some of their new cards. I pointed out what I did not like, what I did not want, and expressed a preference for a higher quality item we had seen elsewhere. Because they carried a fear of being in the company of a negative-thinking person, my friend interpreted my discrimination and seeing of contrast as being "negative." Instantly, they experienced a bad thought-feeling, and verbally judged me to be negative.

When I looked perplexed, we began to speak about it, and then both of us saw the mirror and in that moment we both simultaneously realized that *they* were being negative—*they* were actually creating the very negativity that they did not want to have in their experience.

This happened before I discovered how to be self-fulfilling through the power of love and joy, but the simultaneous mutual recognition and knowing enabled me to not be hurt by the apparent judgment*. To the contrary, I was highly impressed with my friend and thankful for the clear seeing—being open and aware is a wonderful gift that enables truth and love!

There is no problem with other that is not self.

What you fear (inside) appears (outside). Projection is perception, perception is projection. If you are challenged with something similar, do not simply accept the negative feeling and thought as true. Do the practice of *Alchemy* to know non-attachment and to clear your vision.

{ You can't depend on your eyes when your
imagination is out of focus. ~ Mark Twain }

Your mind-reads about others are *your* thoughts. They are your fears, your hopes, projected. But when you see the mirror, you find freedom.

JUDGMENT IS YOUR FEAR, NOT TRUTH

When you are feeling the effect of a negative thought-feeling, do not believe it is true. When you are feeling bad, seek joy first and *then* look again.

If you do not remember to give yourself what you want, then at least question your mind-read. In the example situation above, my friend had to have had some negative mind-read, perhaps something like "She is judging my new cards" perhaps followed by something like "How negative!" Had my friend asked me the purpose of my statements, it would have been known that I was considering my own print project and the quality I wanted to have, and that I was seeking a high quality printer appropriate for the job. It would have been known how *positive* I am.

{ We don't see things the way they are.
We see things the way we are. ~ Talmud }

Better yet, they could have been self-fulfilling. From a good state, my positive purpose and state of mind may have become obvious to them on their own, because that is what *was* and because my friend knew the connection between discussing the design of those cards and the project I was working on. In other words, they knew the context of my thinking, but that and judgment were unknowingly clouded by a bad feeling.

There is a saying that when you make a fist and point one finger, there are three fingers pointing back at you. Judging someone says nothing about them, and much about you.

When we judge something or someone we "freeze" it or them in time, frozen, as if an unchanging truth—but only in our minds because, of course, you can't freeze the ever-changing reality or people. It is our minds that become frozen.

{ When you judge another, you do not define them,
you define yourself. ~ Wayne Dyer }

When we limit our reality with our minds, we limit our experience. When we say "this is the way it is" or "that is the way he or she is," we are saying it is carved in stone. We are saying it's over. Well, it's never over ladies and gentlemen, because *the fat lady never sings*. It's never over because of course we can never limit reality or people. Both are vast and ever-changing regardless of what you think about them.

However, if someone else has not yet found their freedom, judgment can negatively affect them, and certainly your relationship with them. Judgment kills love within you instantly, and what you lose inside, you ultimately lose on the outside.

{ What you are, the world is. And without your transformation, there can be no transformation of the world. ~ J. Krishnamurti }

Belief in a self that needs to struggle and suffer this world serves to hide truth and beget beliefs that we must suffer. But even that is not true—you do not have to suffer, no matter what. What if you could blow out the belief that has held you captive all your life?

CHAPTER 15

Belief in Suffering

What if we believed there was a faster end to suffering? Our society has for generations held and lived the belief that emotion, especially suffering from grief and loss, must be experienced for a certain length of time before one can "release" it and begin to feel better. In reality there is nothing held, so there is nothing to release. We just need to stop repeating suffering. How? Consider that we never really stop anything—we just do something else. Look for, feel for, and *seek* a better feeling.

Left to their own devices, grief and loss will move through on their own. Interfered with by beliefs about how long they should take, it turns into suffering that could become perpetual.

Time does not heal. Time does not change things. Movement does. You don't need time to feel joy. It's a movement you can make now, any now. Every now.

Suffering is like a switch: It is either on or off. So the end of suffering is now. Or not. It cannot be in any other time. After you have met your imagined, suffering-time belief, you will stop suffering, and it will be now. You will begin to know good feeling again. I clearly remember the first several instances, after three months of suffering after Dad passed, when I noticed thoughts like, "Oh, I guess I can enjoy this (event/circumstance/good feeling)" and then I "allowed" myself to do so by keeping my attention on it.

BELIEF IN MOURNING

So we suffer for as long as we believe we "should." This suffering belief is particularly true in the case of the death of a loved one. Not to suffer, or to not suffer long enough, was thought of as disrespectful, or as an indication of a lesser degree of love.

Do you think your deceased one wants you to suffer? If you did not suffer would it mean you love them any less? While suffering, can you give love? Suffering does not equal love. Would your deceased loved one prefer that you experience, have, and "send" them love? You can miss someone or love them, but you can only do one of these at a time.

Your loved one is not here in body, and at some time when that is still true—in a moment when you are forgetting to feel bad—your natural good-feeling state will be known. When you notice it, you may judge it as too early or you will decide to feel good. When do you decide it's time and "okay" to feel good? That time is different for everyone. It has nothing to do with being able or unable, or "having to" mourn. In some societies death is celebrated!

BELIEF IN DEATH

What if they have it right? I mean, consider that in the womb before birth, you are warm, safe, comfortable, fed, and in a quiet place; there is nothing you need. Then without being consulted, you are forced out, violently, into a harsh, glaring, cold, wet, hungry, loud place, grabbed by legs and arms, slapped on the bottom, and *gasp*—now you must breathe in!

With death, eventually there is a release, a quiet letting go, and the final breath is a relaxing "out" breath; it is effortless. These things we know, and yet we revere birth and try to deny death. I am playing with this to restore a little balance; to illustrate how severe and divisive our thinking has been with regard to birth being good and death being bad. In truth, without death there is no birth.

Ironically, people who have been "regressed" to remember birth describe it much like those who had a near-death experience, including going through a black tunnel and seeing a bright light. It's good to wonder about life and death, and in particular about second-hand beliefs that you have never questioned.

In this society people tend to mourn someone who has passed—but did you mourn them before they were born? If they are back where they were before they were born, what is there to mourn? What if, at a funeral, instead of mourning death (which we don't even know anything about), we celebrated life?

{ To fear death is nothing other than to think oneself wise when one is not. For it is to think one knows what one does not know. No one knows whether death may not even turn out to be the greatest blessing for a human being; and yet people fear it as if they knew for certain that it is the greatest evil. ~ Socrates }

If people were completely truthful with themselves, we'd see that we do not really mourn someone else, but rather we are coming face to face with our own mortality and fears, and unfounded beliefs and ideas of an end—or worse, a torturous end.

Standing at my father's casket during a wake and seeing his body, it struck me as odd. Whatever *that* was, it was not him. "It's unreal," I said.

"Yeah," said a family member beside me.

Wanting to clarify that it was not unreal that it happened, but instead, "That's not him...I don't know where he is, but that's not him."

"Oh, I don't have *those* beliefs," they answered just before breaking down. That struck me and I thought "*Oh, but I don't have* those *beliefs,*" and in that moment I realized that people who think they don't have "those" beliefs think that they don't have beliefs. But they are the biggest believers! They believe in birth as a "start" and death as an "end" even though they have no idea what lies before or after either side (or even in the middle), and as a result of these beliefs, they live in fear of death.

{ You don't remember being born, you don't know when you are going to die—do you even know what is here right now? ~ Katie Davis }

{ Die happily and look forward to taking up a new
and better form. Like the sun, only when you set in the west
can you rise in the east. ~ Rumi }

JOY DOES NOT NEED PAIN

Some people believe they need suffering to know joy, but in reality, where is there suffering in joy? You can only know one at a time. If you lived in joy from this day forward, do you really think you will ever forget what suffering is? Have you had enough?

Suffering does not do you, your body, or the people around you any good at all. There is only one purpose for suffering—to wake you up and point you toward joy. Suffering is a choice, usually an unconscious one, which can now be made conscious.

The practice of *The Alchemy of Love and Joy*™ can be used to awaken your self to the choice of suffering. It will work faster when you drop the belief that you must suffer for a long time— and fastest when you drop the belief that you must suffer at all. In every possible moment, there are both reasons to suffer and reasons to rejoice available.

You will prove this with each experience you have of feeling better and better. Having gone through the proverbial six inches of fear in dropping the separated sense of "self," I can testify that what is on the other side feels immensely better than what we thought we were protecting—and it is astronomically better than suffering.

For this purpose, joy is anything that does not feel bad. "Better" does not necessarily mean joyously happy; it just means better than what you were feeling. Just taking your attention off the bad thought-feeling is better.

You don't need to struggle with thoughts and beliefs to feel better now. You just need to pay attention to what you are feeling, and pay attention to what you *do* want and to how that feels. When you do that, because you are not your thoughts and they were never attached to you in the first place, negative thoughts and suffering will fall away.

YOU CAN ALLOW YOURSELF TO FEEL BAD

There is nothing inherently wrong with any of our emotions (the "good" or "bad" ones); they are all just experiences that come and go. It is the unconscious experience of feeling states that can rob you of your life because while unconsciously suffering, we shut down, tend to suffer harder and longer, and act poorly, often hurting others and then later regretting it. We are not present to the effects of our suffering and not present to our life.

Suffering can also cause illness and can lead to an earlier experience of death. An alternative use of your time here would be to experience the possibilities that life without attachment offers.

SUFFER CONSCIOUSLY

Of course it is certainly valid to choose to allow yourself to feel bad. My suggestion is, if that is your choice (or during a moment when that is your experience), to be aware *consciously* that that is what is happening, and to choose the location (and even time), and to not shut down your attention or shut out the whole of the rest of experience, which is always going on.

Closing your eyes when crying shuts out yet more of your body, surroundings, and the rest of reality, so open-eyed crying can help ground you in your body and help you stay aware of everything else going on that is not suffering. Reality was there before, will be there during, and will be there after suffering, so you can use it at any point.

These steps and this awareness will ensure that you are at least conscious of the suffering, and aware of the effect of your actions on others, and that you have the opportunity that such space affords to perhaps not suffer as long or hard, and to know the other possibilities that are available.

If you are going to do it, don't wallow in it, feeding the "poor me" sense of separation. Instead, suffer intentionally, *consciously*, and hard, on purpose, and then watch what happens. Suffering is by nature unconscious, so by bringing consciousness to what you are doing, you will burn through it fast, or even bypass it.

Whether you are feeling good or bad, do it consciously. Knowing presence is key.

BREAK THROUGH

A breakthrough from old patterns takes the determination that I know you must have, since you have found the option to seek joy. The old habits may create struggle, flip-flopping for a while between suffering and feeling good. (But if you changed quickly and easily, I could not stop you!)

Persist in every moment to hold in mind and cultivate what *is* wanted. Deny any and all thought-feelings that do not feel better, that do not move you forward. Deny by noticing and ignoring them, and noticing and picking up something that *does* feel better.

Even if it takes twenty or sixty minutes to shift and become established in relief, then joy or peace, is that better than hours of suffering? Better than feeding the overall habit of suffering? Better than suffering unconsciously for years? A lifetime? You can help speed the breakthrough by changing your body's physiology: stand up, walk, jump, run or play music. But most importantly, hold attention on the thought-feeling of what you *do* want.

Make how you are feeling your highest priority. Having things, people, or events is not a problem, and not having things, people, or events is not a problem. Attaching how we feel to having or not having them *is* a problem. How do you detach? You must want to feel good more than you want (or don't want) the person, event, or thing outside and then put your attention on it to shift the state.

There is certainly a lot of incentive to do so, including immediate relief, possibly pleasure, and freedom from anything outside of you ever hurting you again; safety, security, and peace. And ultimately, love.

Do you really want to feel better
more than you want something outside?

What is key is being truthful—with yourself. For example, with some people who I've guided to feel better, just moments after they begin to feel better, they start to feel bad. What they didn't notice was that a bad thought-feeling arose, and they put their attention on it—right in the middle of feeling good.

People look directly at me, through teary eyes or pained expressions, and answer that they do want to feel better. If that were true for them, they'd stay with the better feeling they just had. Busted with that, the next time, they do stay with it. This realization is a powerful one because now they *know*; one minute they were feeling good, and then the next they were not. Seeing it arise as it happens is a potent way to realize the true cause of pain.

HOW TO HELP SOMEONE ELSE WHO IS GRIEVING

Be still. Be presence—as a verb—as in feeling into the body and breath. Hug them, hold them, if that is welcomed. Help with physical needs and allow the grief to move through without interference, one way or the other. Do not tell them how they should feel, or when they should stop grieving.

If you feel your own suffering beginning to well-up, go inside and give yourself what you want; it will allow space for them to be as they are, and as they will be, and to enable you to be fully there for them if and when they want you.

BLOW OUT THE BELIEF THAT HAS HELD YOU CAPTIVE ALL YOUR LIFE

Blow out the belief that has held you captive all your life; the belief that any thing outside can hurt you or make you feel good. Use suffering as the gift it is. Even as you notice you are feeling bad—*and this is critical*—accept it as an opportunity, a shot at freedom! Do the practice: ask yourself what you want and look, feel, listen, and sense for a better feeling. After you have latched onto it, build it up and when at its peak, ask, "Who or what did I need to feel this?"

Then sustaining the good feeling, look back and notice the situation or circumstance that you used to believe could hurt you; and notice whether it has any power. Realize in this moment that you are the cause of good feeling, in spite of the situation, *and that both co-exist.*

If your energy drops at all while doing this, start over and build it up again, and look back again. It gets easier each time. Don't be concerned if suffering tries to return; just do the practice again. Each time you watch old-mind arise, and you see it as separate from you, each time that you experience seeing that it or circumstances can exist without suffering, *you are eroding the core painful belief* that triggered it. And you are re-affirming knowing your inherent joy. Use the power of *Alchemy* repeatedly until you can see, hear, feel, sense or know both the situation *and* good feeling simultaneously.

Then, still sustaining feeling good, notice the option to suffer; if you feel drawn into it, notice *that is not what you want*, and quickly flip back to the joy. (I discovered that looking into a mirror during this exercise helps in a so far inexplicably, amazing way.) Do this repeatedly until you clearly know and see the suffering as separate, as an option, and *not* as mandatory. You may burst out laughing. You are realizing your freedom. It is a joyous thing.

One client described this process as "learning to walk again." Just like learning to walk, where you flip back and forth between walking and falling down, you flip back and forth between suffering and joy. Eventually, you walk more than fall.

Eventually, you stay with joy more than suffering because you get better at it, and due to your interest in and desire for good feeling. That is when you know walking feels better and takes you farther and faster than crawling. Like falling down, suffering is never a problem, *unless* you stay there.

{ Our greatest glory is not in never falling,
but in rising every time we fall. ~ Confucious }

Once you have known, realized, and actualized the existence of both options, and you experientially know suffering and joy like you experientially know cold or hot, then you have found your freedom. You will know the fundamental untruth in statements like "He hurt me" or "It's a stressful job." You will know that it is you who hurts you, you who stresses you, and you will know you don't have to do these things again.

And yet, there is a purpose for suffering.

CHAPTER 16

Is There a Purpose for Suffering?

Suffering causes you mental and physical anxiety, raises your blood pressure, makes your heart work harder and faster than it needs to, triggers inappropriate and extended adrenaline production, exhausts you, negatively affects the chemistry of the mind, drives you to behave in ways you may regret, and can lead to depression. Suffering strains the body and causes illness. Suffering spreads energetically to other people. It could be called the "greatest" disease, perhaps even the cause of all disease: the disease of all diseases.

{ You will not be punished for your anger;
you will be punished by your anger. ~ The Buddha }

Suffering, be it anger or sadness, drains the body. Yet some people argue that they feel sad on purpose, to support friends. You may be consciously aware that you feel sad in the presence of a friend's sadness. But you can't ever be sad enough to help someone who is feeling sad, and it is not your sadness that helps anyway, it's your better feeling and clarity that does.

To help, you may give space, empathy, or compassion with the intention of helping someone to feel better, by directing someone toward something more beneficial, or offering some suggestion to help someone be more resourceful to deal with sadness or issues. You cannot do this if you are truly as sad, sadder, or unconsciously sad.

Unconscious sadness, or sadness for the sake of wallowing in sadness, serves no beneficial purpose whatsoever. People have asked, "We are human, aren't we meant to experience the full range of emotions?" I would ask: Meant to? By whom?

"They?"

"They," the same people who told you that you were a tiny, powerless being born to suffer, be judged, and die? (And that you were limited in other ways also?)

But, you *are* powerful, *so* powerful that, yes, you can choose to suffer, if that is what you want. No one can take that away. My question to you would be: "For what purpose?"

One day I was walking in the woods when some sad thought which I was only vaguely aware of arose; and a feeling of sadness began to grow. Old-mind would have instantly and habitually begun to search for (and create) the "why I should feel this sadness." Because I no longer automatically believe suffering thoughts nor seek proof to support them, and because I was experimenting with this, the thought "Huh, maybe I could feel sad. I could feel sad, yes I could do that," came instead.

Then, as I began to feel into the body and experience sadness, the question, "and for what purpose?" arose repeatedly. I dug and dug, but could not find one truthful good "sad reason." As sure as I was aware of the little bit of sadness, in my search for a purpose to wallow in it, I was also aware of the trail and birds and bright sun beaming: I was aware of everything else that was also going on, which was not sad.

The sadness did not grow, but instead faded away as a grin spread across my face, and happiness a hundred times the strength of the sadness blossomed, sending chills down my body. All of this happened in moments.

YES, SUFFERING HAS A PURPOSE—TO POINT YOU TOWARDS JOY

The only purpose for suffering is to bring to your attention the direction you are moving, and to point you toward love and joy. When you replace the fundamental root of suffering, which is fear, with its opposite, love; you will come to know you are much more than fear.

When you become aware of it, you can use suffering for the only thing it is good for: to wake up to joy. When you decide to care about how you feel, and you decide to feel good above all else, then you take control of your life, your health, and your contribution to the health and happiness of the world today.

PAIN IS MANDATORY, SUFFERING IS OPTIONAL

{ …pain is mandatory suffering is optional. ~ The Dalai Lama }

"Pain is mandatory; suffering is optional" is often quoted and it sounds reasonable, but how is that so? How is it lived? Pain, physical bodily pain, is a function of the body. Emotional suffering, for psychological "reasons," or in addition to physical pain, is a practice, a habit that can be changed.

THE MECHANICS OF HOW PAIN IS MANDATORY AND SUFFERING IS OPTIONAL

- Pain is a beneficial function of the body, to guide you away from something not beneficial, like a hot stove. Keeping your hand on the stove will keep your hand hurting. Once the body has been hurt, it will continue to hurt until you remove the source of pain and give it rest long enough to heal. This is not optional.

- Suffering is a function of attention, to guide you away from thinking that is painful and not beneficial. Keeping your attention on the pain of suffering will keep it hurting. Unlike the pain of bodily injury, emotional pain stops the moment you move away from it—which means you move toward something that feels better. This is optional.

Any feeling, thought, or belief that is not in alignment with who you naturally are and your innate freedom, love, and joy, will cause suffering to you.

If there is a knife (something outside) sticking out of your arm, you will need to remove it to stop the pain. Perhaps this is where and why we evolved the habit of looking for relief outside. But the pain of emotional suffering is caused by an internal knife, so the cure is inside.

Suffering is something done habitually, something that has been handed down, inherited through simply not knowing what else to do. It can become so deeply ingrained as to become a belief, or worse, a part of our identity (also a belief). You know it's gone that far when you hear people say things like, "I am just a sad person."

The good news is that the same mechanism that can perpetuate bad feeling, suffering, and related beliefs, can be used with the same success to create the habit of relief and the habit of joy, along with their related beneficial beliefs.

What we do habitually becomes what we believe. What we believe becomes what we do habitually. Beliefs change all the time, usually unconsciously. When you take conscious control of your beliefs and habits, and you care about how you feel, you take conscious control of your life.

Choose how you want to be, put your interest in only that and immerse your attention in what you *do* want. Care about how you feel in every moment; be aware of choosing the things you do, read, and listen to, and the people you spend time with. Practice, live, breathe what you do want.

Most importantly, and if you do nothing else, notice and feel emotional pain as a red flag and pay attention! Notice it, and if you don't want the pain, ask yourself what you *do* want, and feel inside for that, because as true as you can always find pain and something to suffer over, you can also always find joy, peace, happiness, love, or connection to "suffer" over. After all, suffering is really just re-experiencing something over and over, often with a building intensity.

Practicing *The Alchemy of Love and Joy*™ gives you the feeling you want that will end painful suffering almost instantly. The question is: Have you had enough? Do you care about how you feel? Do you care about how you act? Do you really want change? Do you really want happiness, peace, joy? But don't believe me that it's possible. Try it on yourself and practice joy moment to moment to see, feel, and know.

JOY IN SICKNESS

For the first time since learning how to awaken joy, I felt physically sick, and the phenomenon was fascinating. It may have been the orange juice and iron pill that triggered the "pained feeling" in my stomach, which became an overall feeling of sickness so quickly that I did not notice the switch—until I began the practice.

As I laid down in bed, about to succumb to the sick feeling that was beginning to spread all over, it occurred to me to see what would happen if I practiced. As I went inside to seek a better feeling, it was like the overall "sickness feeling" physically separated from the stomach pain and "lifted." As the good feeling grew, the "sickness feeling" faded, disappeared, and then even the stomach pain felt far away. When I stopped practicing, the "sickness feeling" returned! So I continued feeling good (while noticing the distant stomach pain), and fell asleep with a smile.

When you have a physical illness or challenge, do you think that it is more beneficial to feel emotionally good, or bad? Feeling good may actually be quite important to the healing of the body, and your condition is an excellent opportunity to drop the belief that anything outside you can make you feel bad. Accepting the situation and recognizing you are going to go through it anyway, why not use it to see what is genuinely possible?

Physical pain is an important message from your body. Be thankful for it and listen to it. Mental and emotional pain will not help the body, and over time will harm it.

Learn to differentiate the two so that you can act accordingly, and prevent yourself from becoming another statistic.

CHAPTER 17

Radical Reversal of Expert Self-Help Advice

THE STATS ON DEPRESSION

In spite of all the well-intentioned "traditional" advice:

- One in ten U.S. adults report depression. (Centers for Disease Control and Prevention, CDC, 2008)
- For youth and young adults between the ages of 10 and 24, suicide is the third leading cause of death. (Centers for Disease Control and Prevention, CDC, 2004)
- "...the U.S. suicide rate has climbed steadily since 1999, driven by an alarming increase among middle-age adults." (Los Angeles Times, Oct. 21, 2008)
- Child depression drug use has quadrupled in a decade (BBC News, 2007 "GPs in England wrote more than 631,000 such prescriptions for children in the last financial year, compared to just 146,000 in the mid-1990s.")
- 15% of preschoolers struggle with depression and anxiety. (Journal of Child Psychology and Psychiatry, 2009)

Children! At the most playful, positive, and free time in their lives, children are now a high-risk, highly prescribed group. With these increasing statistics, should we not be looking skeptically at what we are doing?

The brain has natural pain relievers (endorphins) and mood stabilizers (serotonin) that are affected by diet, exercise, and relaxation. Laughter (and probably joy) triggers the brain to produce endorphins, lowers blood pressure, reduces stress hormones, improves circulation, boosts the immune system, oxygenates the blood, and gives a sense of well-being.

When suffering, none of this is possible, and may in fact be reversed. Should we not be prescribing the natural healing power of the body-mind--for adults and children? Should we not start tapping into joy, for both prevention and treatment? Should we not be questioning and dropping old beliefs that do not work? Should we not be teaching joy?

{ Norman Cousins, who later in life suffered from a form of arthritis (or possibly reactive arthritis) developed a recovery program incorporating mega doses of Vitamin C, along with a positive attitude, love, faith, hope, and laughter induced by Marx Brothers films. "I made the joyous discovery that ten minutes of genuine belly laughter had an anesthetic effect and would give me at least two hours of pain-free sleep," he reported. "When the pain-killing effect of the laughter wore off, we would switch on the motion picture projector again and not infrequently, it would lead to another pain-free interval." He wrote about these experiences in several books. ~ Wikipedia }

CURRENT PSYCHOLOGY AND DEPRESSION

The majority of self-help experts still speak as if outside things make us happy. They recommend that you, "Do things that make you happy." Not only are they missing the mark, they are actually pointing you away from it. "Things" do not "make" you happy and "things" do not "make" you unhappy. You can walk through a flower garden feeling miserable just as much as you can walk through one feeling joy. On the walk, you may be distracted from the suffering and that may give you space for joy. It may happen. Then again, it may not. Without an interest in feeling better and without presence, your experience will be left totally up to the busy, slippery mind and wandering attention.

There are salt water tanks designed to mimic the stillness and peace of being in the womb, with controlled temperature and so much salt that you float. You can pay good money to be there and still be lost in a stressful stream of thinking the whole time. If you have not practiced some form of stillness, of meditation or slowing the mind, or *Alchemy*, then I would not recommend the tank experience, as I have seen people come out of it in worse shape than they went in; more stressed *and* claustrophobic.

No matter what you are doing, or where you are, how you feel depends on what your attention is on and what your interest is in. Usually though, most people are unconsciously re-churning more of the same old stories and pain.

The end objective of all self-help expert advice is ultimately for you to feel good. The methods or actions (e.g., walking) are not the results (e.g., feeling). They never have been and never will be. A walk does not guarantee good feeling. However, you can go right to the feeling you want, walking or sitting.

Recognizing that there is a thought-feeling connection, self-help experts also say to "control your thoughts," yet several also know and teach that you can't control your thoughts. Ever try to force a good thought on a bad feeling? If so, you know it doesn't work, and it may even hurt more. This is why people are saying that *The Alchemy of Love and Joy*™ is the missing key. It is the radical opposite; you feel good *first*, then good thoughts follow easily and naturally.

Neurology of feeling

Repeated experiences of suffering may enable you to become neurologically better at suffering. In the body, nerve cells pass signals from one to the other. When one cell repeatedly assists in firing another cell by sending a signal to it, part of that cell modifies for better connection. (See http://en.wikipedia.org/wiki/Hebbian_theory).

From the discovery of this Hebbian Theory came the saying, "what fires together, wires together," which means that nerve cells repeatedly stimulated in a certain pattern increase their synaptic (nerve cell) strength for that pattern, building "neural networks," (systems of cells) for that purpose. In other words, the body physically re-wires itself to better generate the pain of suffering. (This mechanism is also perhaps how athletes can become so highly, unconsciously competent at what they do.)

This does not mean that you cannot do or choose something different; it's just that it is easier to do what you have already repeatedly done. The good news is that this conditioning to do something well is called "synaptic *plasticity*" for a reason: it can be changed. We are always re-wiring ourselves, consciously or unconsciously. Anger makes you better at feeling angry, which feels bad. What do you want to be good at?

The reverse of depression

"Depressions" may begin with negative thoughts and beliefs which create bad feeling, which perpetuates negative thoughts, until the cycle becomes deeply conditioned, and intense suffering over time can alter the chemistry of the brain and its neurological function. You can see how things can spiral downward. *The Alchemy of Love and Joy*™ practice uses that same body-mind "function" but in reverse, to create the opposite of depression—habitual joy.

Nothing, no thing, is depressing, except a thought-feeling you can access. So, seek a better feeling—*seek joy!*

VENTING AND SUPPRESSION

"But what about all the experts who say to 'vent' your feelings?" a client asked me. My reply was, "How well did that work?" So, here you are, still seeking peace, freedom, and joy.

You don't need to vent (i.e., re-create) feelings to "release" them. They are not stuck or attached to you—you continually re-create, re-live and perpetuate them. Just a tiny step better than suppressing bad feeling, "venting" and "releasing" implies suppression, and could create a more intense experience of the pain. Venting does not guarantee suffering will not return. (In fact, it likely *will* return since the attachment and belief that you used to create it have not changed and by repeatedly venting, you get better at it.)

In addition, because there is a belief that after venting the emotion will "release," you do release. *You* release. (i.e., you chose to move your attention from where it was and put it on something better). Why not skip the intensity and just go straight to the "*you release?*"

I have personally experienced the fact of this choice, in relationships, but also in a brush with a serious car accident. The icy road and pouring rain had most cars moving cautiously in both lanes that night. Out of the corner of my eye I caught sight of a speeding blur and suddenly a red car was right in front of me, spinning. I thought, "Both of us cannot lose control," and the last vague thought was, "Stay in control."

I kept my eye on the front end of that car as it spun around, and every time it came toward me it sped up, and when it went away, it slowed down. Every time it came toward me there was a wordless knowing that "this could be it," and I became extremely aware and highly present. But mind was no where to be found. There was complete control and utter stillness as I gently braked and gradually geared down. Then the car went back into the right lane, still spinning, and it seemed it was over, at least for me, but a moment later it came back in front again, still spinning. Once again, I began gingerly breaking, as I eyed the nose, knowing multiple times where it must have missed me by an inch or less. Finally, the car spun away again, regained control, and astonishingly to me, just kept going.

Thoughts began to rush back in, like, "Oh my god! I could have been killed! How could he just keep going?" The nervous system does not know the difference between imagined peril and true peril, and it responds to thoughts of peril. So with that, anxiety began to rocket and I pulled over to the side of the road, shaking with panic. Then the absurdity hit me. *I am panicking now*? I am perfectly fine and safe right now. (But I would not have wanted to panic then, either, and was thankful for the stillness).

When I was in danger I was beyond calm, I was utterly still. That is what being here and now is. The thought, "I could have been killed," is the past, and in actuality, it is really nothing. It never happened, and it was not happening now. But with the believed thought "I could have been killed," the body swung into high gear with bodily anxiety, which in turn spun the mind for a while, and it took me some time to calm down enough to drive again.

It seems the body does not know about the linguistic future, it only knows now, and so recognizes and interprets that there is danger now when the mind shouts a past or future red alert that is believed now.

{ Imagination, because of having freedom from external limitations, can often become a source of real pleasure and unnecessary suffering. Consistent with this idea, imagining pleasurable and fearful events is found to engage emotional circuits involved in emotional perception and experience. See: http://en.wikipedia.org/wiki/Imagination }

On some level, after the car regained control, when there was still stillness, before mind stepped in and before panic had consumed the body, I knew I did not have to pull over, and yet there was some belief that I "should" be scared, and so I became scared when I was perfectly safe. Absurd.

Many times I have heard people tell stories about how something happened, and about how they could not explode where they were, under certain circumstances or with certain people around, and so they had to "hold it back" until later. What does that say? It says they were in control, they were deciding whether they could explode or not, and where and when. Believing you need to vent can lead to abusive behaviors and cycles.

ABUSE IS CONFUSION

Consider that the commonplace belief in (and "acceptance" of) "needing to vent" may be a factor in abusive cycles. Abusive people, who first believe they should feel bad and then angry, and then that they must suppress it (not knowing what else to do), then think they need to "release" it, and then can feel correct or right in so doing—and the angry behavior is usually directed at someone else. These beliefs stem from the core belief that something or someone else is the cause of how we feel. When you recognize the true cause as within yourself, all stacked beliefs tumble, you cannot hurt others, and compassion and empathy can come to life.

In the case of abusive patterns, attachment beliefs are so strong that the abuser completely dissociates from responsibility and empathy, enabling them to selectively attach their anger to whomever they have come to believe can (and perhaps should) alleviate it, and is therefore responsible for it. (Note that they do not abuse everyone.) Believing these distorted thoughts, they will alter their reality to support their beliefs, seeing or creating many "reasons" and justifications for their controlling behavior and abuse. Like the rest of society, but to an extreme, highly emotional degree, they confuse love with need and blame their pain on someone outside themselves.

Whether you are navigating depression or anger, both are based on confusion and attachment. *The Alchemy of Love and Joy*™ is a bridge that can help people go beyond conditioned beliefs and confusion.

And whether you are navigating depression or anger, both have the same positive intention and purpose: love, joy, and peace. It's just that the attachment and outer need method has not worked and can never work—*it will always backfire*, if not immediately, then eventually.

When you ask yourself what you want and answer with your whole body-mind, you are moving to the other side, away from attachment and need, away from blame, away from false comfort, and toward *true* and lasting love, joy, and peace.

The knee-jerk, self-ish response to bad feeling is much like a mindless itch you scratch, except that this is poison ivy of the mind, and the more you scratch, the worse it gets. The more you believe the outside is responsible, the more "it will bother you," and there is no relief in sight. This is the current human condition that may well be responsible for depression, aggression, and addiction. Certainly it is responsible for intense pain in relationships, but it can be cured.

CHAPTER 18

You Can't Feel Someone's Love

After weeks of happiness, bliss, and peace, one morning I woke with a dream in memory, and noticed a feeling that was not my norm, not joyful. I dreamt of someone whom I'd like in my life giving attention to someone else. Immediately I began to practice.

"What do I want?"

Hmmm…this took a moment or two as the dream fog began to clear…and then it came:

"I want to feel that person's love."

"How does that person's love feel?"

As I reached for the feeling, wonderful images, smiles, and loving memories flashed; and a warm, tingly sensation began to flow through my body.

"Is this what I prefer to feel?"

"Yesssssss, hehe."

"Who's love did I need?"

"Ohhh mine, and I am so grateful that it is here for me!"

"Feeling this way, how do I act?"

I reflected on the dream again, and this time enjoyed the other's enjoyment, happiness, and interaction *with the other person*. There were no negative feelings of loss or jealousy (that may have been what they were, although I never bothered to get specific or label them), there was just infinite love. The pleasure grew as a smile stretched across my face.

"Is this what I prefer to do, give, or send?"

Definitely—I wanted to experience love, and "offer" or connect with that person with love, even in their absence. As I continued to enjoy those sensations, the overall feeling of love grew, expanded, and enveloped me. I snuggled with pleasure deeper into the pillows and sheets, and my body warmed as if glowing.

The love got better and better, and at the peak I recognized *that this feeling was exactly what it felt like when that person was here*, "giving" (I thought) love "to me." A realization was re-affirmed, and it sunk in:

> *I created the feeling* then, *when they were here,*
> *just as I am creating it* now, *when they are not!*

The cause was not the other person then, as it was not now. *Even the sense of other comes from within you*, whether they are present or not. It is felt in your body-mind. Thinking about that; how could it be any other way? A playful giggle arose, followed closely by laughter. The cosmic joke is so much fun. Who's love did I need? Mine. It was my love that I have only ever had or wanted.

Oh yes, and what of that bad feeling I awoke with? Long gone and long forgotten! Lingering longer in bed, I savored the love and then a growing bliss from experiencing a yet larger expansion: there was no more subject or object of love; it was just pure love. Joining the others in the kitchen, my great big grin and the all-over warmth persisted for hours into the morning. I wondered what they thought.

Enjoy your self—Self *is* all *you ever do enjoy!*

Two people can celebrate love the emotion, express its presence, see expression of it in each other's faces, and hear symptoms of it in the other's voice, but you cannot feel the other's love. You just feel *your love*, in your body-mind. The love they feel is theirs—in, through, and with their body-mind. As well, no one can "withhold" the feeling of love from you. No matter their actions or inactions, you can always feel love.

{ Nobody can take themselves from me.
They don't have that power! ~ Byron Katie }

IT'S EASY TO PROVE THAT YOU ARE THE SOURCE OF LOVE

You do know what skin and bones feels like, right? OK, take one hand and touch the top of the other one with it, feeling what skin and bones feels like. That's right, it feels hard and soft and bumpy.

Now feel it with *love*.

OK, I'll let you enjoy that for a bit.

At first it's briefly in the hand and fingers, and then as you enjoy that, you'll notice it grows and expands, moving through the body and maybe beyond. Enjoy the love.

In the same way that you can't feel someone's love, the forgiveness of others does not exist.

CHAPTER 19

The Forgiveness of Others Does Not Exist

One day, a slight "off" feeling stuck around my solar plexus for a few moments. I had not been "off" much since discovering joy—the gift of suffering does not last long as it is just a pointer toward joy, which I gratefully accept. I knew the feeling was related to someone else from my past about whom I had been thinking, and so I began the practice.

"What do I want?"

Hmmmm. I tried on a few things like "to love that person" and "to feel that person's love," but this time these things did not match. Nothing filled the gap, until I hit on wanting that person's forgiveness. Old-mind began to arise,

"But they won't even speak to you, how can you have their forgiveness…?"

Ignoring that thought, which did not feel good and was designed to take me in the wrong direction toward suffering, I continued with the practice. (Remember: We do not want the thing, person, or event—we want the *feeling* we mistake them for.)

"How does their forgiveness feel?"

Wow! The match was perfect, the connection and the feeling were immediate and so powerful, so overwhelming, that they brought tears of joy. There was instant relief, and beyond that, lightness and happiness. I could have enjoyed and explored this for quite some time if I wasn't so compelled to write about the experience and the intelligent recognitions that were coming with it.

Old-mind would have me believe that since that person will not speak with me, they do not want to forgive, and that I cannot have their forgiveness. But I know that mind-reads like that are old-mind's trap, its illusion, its effort to find "proof" in support of a "reason" to suffer, to make the option of suffering actually into an experiential reality.

Instead of asking, "Why do I feel like this?" which only serves to substantiate suffering, I used suffering as a cue to seek relief, to seek joy—because I know it is always there. To be able to know a problem, you must know the solution. To be able to know (experience) "pain," then its opposite, "joy," must also be there.

When feeling better, a vast intelligence is available, one that is not self-centered and suffering-centered. Thoughts that could be as true, or truer, can then be known. Like the fact that healthy, happy, caring people don't act this way, so it is more likely that the person *can't* speak to me, which would indicate *they* are unwell or suffering in some way. Now compassion kicks in. And of course, having sought a better feeling and *experienced* forgiveness, I know there is no way that I cannot have forgiveness. So much clarity and sanity come with feeling good.

The feeling of "lack of forgiveness" (or of being responsible, at fault, etc.) is like any other feeling, *created within*. Thus, the anti-dote, "feeling forgiveness," exists within. If the other person were ever able to bless themselves enough to offer verbal forgiveness to me on the outside, the feeling of forgiveness *must still arise from within me*, because even if they forgave, I could *still* choose to *not* forgive myself and not feel it.

Like all experience, the cause, the source, the origin of the feeling of forgiveness resides within, and *nowhere* else. We actually don't need to hear it from someone to give it to ourselves. Dead or alive, present or absent, we can receive, experience, and enjoy the forgiveness of the "other."

Earlier I described a similar revelation about feeling the love "of another." We say the words, "I want to feel their love" as if the feeling of "the love of another" exists outside us; but in reality, our experience of "their love" is within. It is always only our experience of ourselves. It is *our* love. In the same way, it is *our* forgiveness.

So, I have said:

Enjoy yourself; Self is all you ever do enjoy.

Now I add:

Forgive yourself; you are the only one that can.

(Of course, not as a thought, but as a feeling.)

This complete reversal in experience should come as no surprise to me anymore; however, when the longing or pain is so completely and quickly fulfilled, it is still astonishing, and fully satisfying.

While getting used to this right way of living "inside out" instead of "outside in," there will be more experiences and more integration, in more and more contexts. One of the most powerful is learning to *love before you think.*

CHAPTER 20

Love Before You Think™

In relationships, to "be the change you want to see," is to love before you think. When you think first, then your love is conditional. It says, "I'll feel good when *you* change."

Loving unconditionally is not accepting or "putting up with" things you see that you don't like—it is *not even seeing them* in another. It is refusing to blame another, refusing to blame the outside for what you feel inside. It's choosing to love someone and to love *love* so much that you desire to see only the good in them, and you believe only the best of them. Looking for, supporting, and living only the good in them is one way you create your (and their mutual) reality. To do this—*love yourself first*.

Love yourself fully by giving yourself what you want emotionally so that you are not needy in the relationship; so that you know, experience, and give more than just your wants, needs, and desires; so that you see clearly with open intelligence, and you see something of the truth of everything going on around you, not just your narrow, negative, needy feeling. Do this not just as a concept, not just as the thought, "I love myself" but in action, by going inside and giving yourself what you want when you notice a bad feeling.

Say you are traveling with someone you are getting to know and their behavior is not what you'd like; they are not happy-go-lucky. From your place of feeling dragged down, you may negatively interpret or mind-read (apply meaning to) their behavior.

You may come to some feared conclusion about them, some thought, or some belief, for example, that they don't travel well, or that they are uncomfortable or out of place in new places.

This is how "what you fear appears" and "perception is projection" works. The irony is that in order for you to be a happy traveler, you need something from *them*—you need them to be a happy traveler. This is the "mirror" life is for you. Whatever you are missing (not giving yourself) inside, you will see outside; then you will create dissatisfaction and mistake the cause. You will put conditions on your love. Become the happy traveler yourself, first—after all, *you expected it of them*.

If instead, you gave yourself the feeling you have been denying yourself (for example, the feeling your partner is a good traveler with whom you can happily go anywhere) then your vision and intelligence would open up to the whole of reality, and you might notice the actual person, beyond your fears, beyond your mind-reads, beyond your own negative state.

You might notice they are not feeling well, or that this is not their "usual self," the self you love and believe in, and you might wonder what it is all about for them (instead of believing it is all about what you fear—that they are a bad traveler), and then you might become "other" centered, instead of "self" centered, and you might think to wonder and ask how *they* are.

With that you might learn something of their truth; something of their reality, of their present experience (not just yours)—like maybe something they have not shared with you yet because an intimate opening, a trusting, a safe space, has not yet been created between you, or for whatever other reason. Let them know what you are perceiving, and that you are having a mind-read about it.

You may learn that something happened just before the trip, or that they are short on cash, or they perceive that something else is stressing or bothering them. This may bring you both closer, you may open to compassion, and both of you may connect with true intimacy. You may be the change you want to see: you may feel like the happy, easy traveler that you want, one who cares about your travel mates, and how your partner is feeling. You may *love*, and with that do what you can to help both of you, and your mutual love may deepen.

Don't resist a bad feeling, thereby putting more of your attention into it. Move toward joy; seek joy inside. Your trip could become better than you ever imagined. The trust and intimate, genuine openness that relationships need in order to thrive can be created. What is an opportunity can be made into suffering and loss, or growth and love.

So you have choice and opportunity with every situation to love more or to love less: to choose love over fear and mind-reads; to build a negative fantasy image of your partner in your mind, or to be genuinely open to true intimacy; to suffer or to seek joy so that you are—and live—love.

Feeling good first is useful in all relationships, and it is critical in intimate relationships, particularly in this society where we have confused love with need. To differentiate, we must know what love is, and what it is not.

CHAPTER 21

What is Love?

Some cultures have multiple words for different kinds of love. In North America, we have "one-word-fits-all," but it does not, and so love the *feeling* can become confused with love the *verb*, love the *action*. Love *the decision* is expressed through the loving actions of forgiveness, patience, dedication, commitment, and selfless compassion.

People can say "I love you" and mean to communicate that they are feeling love. It does not necessarily mean that they will not be attached to you being a certain way, and certainly, if someone believes love is merely a feeling, then they *are* attached and the pain of that will eventually surface. "I love you" does not necessarily mean that they are committed to loving you—indeed they may not even know what that is, or how to do it.

The people who think love is merely a feeling will say they have "fallen out of love," which means that because they are not feeling love right now, they do not believe they will feel love again, and they will not act with love now. So they believe they have no choice, however *they have made this decision*.

If you act like you cannot love simply when you are not feeling it, or because you are feeling bad, then your relationships will be a roller coaster ride of ups and downs, dependant on your ever-changing, unreliable, feeling state, and events you attach it to.

As well, it doesn't take time to love someone; you do it now, or not. Love knows no distance, space, or time. If you make the decision to love now, and to be self-fulfilling first, then you know and have eternal love. The decision to love is not made when you say "I do," it is made moment to moment.

UNCONDITIONAL LOVE DOES NOT EXIST

If you hold the idea that you need or want to give unconditional love, then right there it means you have pre-existing conditions (also called attachments). It also means that you do not love, for love and conditions cannot co-exist. So while you look for or strive to love, you miss love and you struggle, instead of simply feeling it. When living in joy, there *are* no conditions, there is just love.

Seek joy, and there is no need for, and not even any such thing as, "unconditional love." You have no need to take or demand, and nothing to protect or defend from others. Seek joy, seek joy, seek joy "within" and there is only love "without."

The love you seek outside has always been inside.

{ Internal and external are ultimately one. When you no longer perceive the world as hostile, there is no more fear, and when there is no more fear, you think, speak and act differently. Love and compassion arise, and they affect the world. ~ Eckhart Tolle }

LOVE IS NOT NEED

Most people in our society think that having the perfect partner will make you happy, and so this is the purpose of their search. Wanting someone else to make you happy means you are *not* happy, or not happy enough, or that you need someone else in order to be truly happy. But need is not love.

Both partners intend on "making" each other happy by being what the other wants. But, "You be this for me, and I'll be that for you…" is *trading*, not love.

Trading, which is need, is a set-up for pain and suffering. So these fledgling relationships are extremely challenged and this is why our relationships have been intensely painful: they inevitably don't fulfill our needs—because they *can't*.

Perhaps it is because we have feared and lived as if we were this tiny, powerless being with limited joy that is controlled by everything and everyone outside of us, that there has been a sense of need. And we have used relationships as an attempt to fulfill our needs.

It is an error to think others are the cause of your happiness (and therefore unhappiness), and to put that responsibility on them. If they can make you happy, then they can make you unhappy. Then you need them or something from them and are attached. Need and attachment are not love. When you are attached, your "love" can turn to anger in a hurry. But in truth, love can never be anger; so this is need.

Our culture is littered with the belief that love is need, and it is even viewed by many as a positive thing, a romantic thing. This is reflected in our most popular songs with lyrics like, "And I need you more than ever!" Songs with these kinds of lyrics, "Will you love me forever, do you need me!?" have made millions or more. Then there are the controlling clichés like, "If you loved me, you'd…" all glaring examples of confusing love with need.

When I began to detach from looking to the outside to fulfill me, initially it became increasingly difficult to enjoy songs, and music had been a large part of my life. Most of them, I found, were about attachment—or so it appeared.

Yet here again the mirror applied. Attachment may (or may not) have been the inspiration to write the songs; however any song can be viewed and experienced with different eyes and heard with different ears from multiple perspectives. Whenever there was a judgment or a separate "you" being accused in the song, I began to experience the "you" not as another person, but as separation (or at the time, ego*) itself. Now I could sing along with any song! Perspective is everything. There are no problems with songs; there is no problem with anything else that is not self.

When you need, you may fear, and fear is the opposite of love. Fear may manifest as judgments and beliefs that will enable you to destroy a relationship that might otherwise be full of love. Being emotionally needed by someone is not a good thing for either partner.

You imagine and fantasize the ideal partner as someone who "completes" you, who meets your every need, and then you think you've met him or her. When reality clashes with your fantasy's demands and you don't see clearly, you will come to believe your partner is the problem. If you just switch partners believing him or her to be the problem then you will never find the solution, and the pattern will repeat itself over and over.

And is switching partners ever deeply fulfilling? New loves may be exciting, early on, but they are roller-coaster rides as the newness wears off and once again you are left looking for love. Deep fulfillment in anything; work, relationships, life, comes from service, from giving, not from "taking or getting" love; it comes from *being* love. Fulfillment and love come from within. If you are always trying to change the outside to get your needs and wants met, you are never in the position to give or feel real, fulfilling love and you are always disturbed by the outside, which is ever changing.

In the "rose colored glasses" early stage of a relationship, hopes are high, so we tend to see the things we are looking for, even if they aren't really there. In the beginning everyone is also on their best behavior and doing everything possible to impress, which cannot and will not last. Each will get comfortable and lapse back into their normal habitual behavior. After that stage, we don't see clearly either—we begin to see the things we fear, even if they aren't really there. If the relationship makes it past these stages, there is an opportunity for the partners to leave need, hope, and fear, trading them for real love.

To know the true source of infinite joy is to be so full of love that you are, have, and give pure love that has no conditions or needs.

Don't seek the perfect partner, seek to see with perfect eyes

Remember that we don't ever experience reality directly; we experience our perception and interpretation of reality, and that perception has been filtered through and influenced by our fears, hopes, beliefs, memories, associations, etc.

To me, this is one way that, "No two people have ever met," as Byron Katie[2] says. Who we meet, time and time again, is ourselves—but only always. We meet our fears, hopes, beliefs, memories, and other "filters." Good thing we have choice inside.

You can destroy a love relationship in the mind—regardless of what you have or don't have on the outside. You may leave love, but love never leaves you and is always available. Awesome relationships don't come from finding the perfect partner, but from seeing your partner with perfect eyes. In that way, two people can co-create an exceptional relationship of love and joy.

Perfect eyes do not allow the dust of negative or limiting beliefs to settle on them. Perception is projection, is your experi-

(²Check out one of my favorite Byron Katie YouTube videos by Googling: "Unconditional love happens in a questioned mind")

ence; you create your partner, your lover. The only useful belief to hold about your partner is that he or she is unlimited, and that is the closest you can come to the truth with a thought.

{ Beauty is not in the face; beauty is a light in the heart.
~ Kahlil Gibran }

Trying to find the "ideal" fixed partner—someone who has every little characteristic you need in order for you to be happy in all circumstances, is impossible. There are just too many opportunities for your perfect, static fantasy to pop—and, you are expecting the outside to make you happy! In your experience, has the outside ever *not* changed? Your perfect partner will change.

Just as likely, from the place that you need someone not to be "X" for you to be happy, you are just waiting, fearing that "X" will happen, so you are looking for "X" to happen, and you will mind-read or imagine seeing "X," and in that way, you will create it.

You will be for me what I believe you to be.
I will be for you what you believe me to be.
In this way, we create our reality.

From a needy, negative place you are negatively motivated. When you are negatively motivated, you cannot have all the information available in order to make the best choices; you are not acting with or through intelligence; you believe one tiny, contracted piece of information, most likely your own petty negativity, over all other possibilities, and over the totality of the reality. You may actually be with an ideal partner, but it will not matter who you are with; in a contracted, narrow state you can't find anything to love.

{ A man sees in the world what he carries in his heart. ~ Goethe }

Even what is considered a "normal" or "healthy" common relationship, the "romantic" relationship, is founded on some sort of need, expectation, trade, or attachment. So the common relationship is all about struggling through swings of ups and downs in a tug of war of conflicting needs. Real love has nothing to do with need exchange. Real love is letting others be, and if necessary, letting others go.

Loving (self-fulfilled) in a partnership does not mean that you won't see contrasts to what you prefer, does not mean that you won't have preferences about the partner or the partnership, or that you won't grow and change yourself, creating new preferences. There may still be quirks you'd rather your partner not have, but these are not problems and cannot interfere with love, and full of self-love, you can even love their quirks.

A genuine love partnership is when both people hold mutual beliefs that they are individually unlimited, appreciate where each other is now, and support each other in co-creating a vision that moves beyond perceived limitations. In a genuine love partnership, self-love and joy are awakened; there is a desire for true intimacy beyond surface personality, beyond need and attachment. There is generous space to just be.

BE LOVE, SO YOU CAN FEEL LOVE

To create an exceptional relationship, you must love yourself first by giving yourself what you want. Only from a self-fulfilled place do you have something to give, only from there can you truly love. Only from there can you allow your partner to be as he or she is. Only from there can you know your partner as bigger, know your partner as unlimited; and give support in that, and get supported in that.

Self-fulfilled, you don't need
—only then can you love "unconditionally"

Find your ideal partner *inside* first. Love that ideal partner completely, give yourself everything. Whatever you want and desire to feel, instead of demanding it come from the outside, use *Alchemy* and give it to yourself inside. Give yourself so much love that you can't contain it, that it spills out from you all over! Become self-fulfilling. Become so full of love that nothing can hurt you and you can hurt no one. Become invincible in, through, with, and *as* love.

{ Falling in love you remain a child; rising in love you mature.
And by and by love becomes not a relationship;
it becomes a state of your being.
Then it is not that you love this and you don't love that, no
—you are simply love. ~ Osho }

Very early on in a new relationship, establish what I call a "sacred space," where, with loving intention, you drop masks; find a safe time and place to share your genuine selves, the honest truth of your reality, experience, state, and mind-reads.

For someone to honestly share their mind-read so that it can be cleared up shows the highest degree of trust, love, and commitment. Knowing that in a negative state your partner is hurting and that their pain and mind-reads are about *them*, not you, you will not be offended by the mind-read, but instead may appreciate it and your partner all the more.

If you notice a reaction to another's state or mind-read, right then and there ask yourself what you want and give it to yourself *before responding*.

Doing this together could have an almost magical effect on the situation. The degree of trust and vulnerability expressed will build a strong foundation, and shared mind-reads will not smolder or be able to feed fears.

If you open yourself this way when getting to know someone and you are not accepted, then you have saved time and can move forward and find someone who can and will love you. If on the other hand you are fully accepted and your partner opens to you, you can relax into your true selves on this new, solid foundation where love is alive.

You have nothing to lose. Be your genuine self.

In self-fulfilled love you can be fully present, accept your genuine selves; you can truly love each other, live in joy; and support each other in truth, freedom, and in self-actualization.

Being self-fulfilled in a relationship is no more or less important than being self-fulfilled when single, because being alone does not mean being lonely.

CHAPTER 22

Alone, and Not Lonely

Alone is a fact, a circumstance.
Lonely is a feeling.
One has nothing to do with the other.

It has been my experience so far that people who are happily part-nered "give and receive" (or more accurately, simply experience) love more often. Singles often think they need a partner to do this, so love and happiness may not be a regular experience for them. But love and happiness are important for good health, and if we do not partake of them regularly, we may also be more susceptible experiencing negative thoughts and feeling.

Single people, or someone in a stale or stalling relationship, can dramatically benefit from this self-enjoyment. Just because there is not someone there to snuggle up with and enjoy feeling good with does not mean that you cannot do it on your own, and when you awaken joy within yourself within in a stale relation-ship, you will be surprised at what may happen. You don't have to wait for the perfect lover (single or partnered). The perfect lover is where they have always been, and where they will only always be—within.

There are many suggestions from self-help experts for activi-ties to bring more love into your life, like listening to music, buying flowers, walking on the beach, spending time with friends, walking pets, having a wonderful meal, gardening, or looking at artwork, but none of these activities matter. You can do any one of those things in a miserable state. What you do "out there" is not the cause of love inside. Your state of body-mind—no matter what you are doing—is the only thing that matters! Making caring how you feel every moment a priority in your life is the only thing that matters—*seek joy!*

Make feeling good a habit and you will experience more love and joy in life. I began doing this as I fall asleep, and as I awoke before getting out of bed.

By practicing *The Alchemy of Love and Joy*™, seeing the magic in life, and seeking joy in every thing, singles can experience just as much—or more—love and happiness as couples.

WARNING: While alone, and especially after a break-up or while your partnership is struggling, be cautious about how you use your friendships. Remember, the best intentions can fail and friends can unwittingly help keep you trapped as a separate, limited being. Yes, there are times when the behavior of friends backfires.

CHAPTER 23

When Friendships Aren't Friendly

In sharing with friends, I encourage you to look closely at your actions and intentions. Are you looking for a sympathetic ear, someone to support your mind-reads and beliefs about others in order to feel better, in order to feel justified? It's interesting that in friendship we often look for verification of our painful, limited thoughts and views. Could that be because deep down, we know they are not inherent truths?

If this is how you use friendships, then you will continue to support the idea of a weak "you" that needs defending; you will keep yourself distant from genuine relationship; you will more deeply ingrain your reasons for blaming the outside, and more deeply ingrain the habit of creating reasons and blame. You will never get to the source of suffering, or to peace.

Are you afraid to look inside? That would be understandable; looking inside when you are feeling bad, without knowing how to feel better, might feel worse, and it might not get you very far. But, when you give yourself what you want, you can look inside fearlessly. To be fearless is not to be brave; it is to know that there is nothing to fear.

If you and your friend do what I and my friend did, and take broader perspectives and question into all your painful thoughts and mind-reads, you may just come to the same conclusion we did: that you can't really know *anything* about *anyone else* for sure.

This left me asking "questionable" persons about their intention or state, if I could. That was at least a step forward.

Now through the practice and self-fulfilled detachment, I simply don't have things to complain about to friends. If needed, I look inside, feel love, and take action, which may mean speaking with the other person and making decisions based on that conversation and my clear seeing. As well as being better for myself and others, it has also freed my friendships up for other, more productive or fun things than using them to complain about others.

Friendships have also been used for venting, which (as I remember) does not leave the "dumped on" friend feeling good or peaceful. If you have friends that after venting leave you "drained," you may want to reconsider how you relate to them. Of course, you can come to know that friends cannot drain you, and when you do, the relationship will naturally change of its own accord because you will no longer have interest in such conversations.

And finally, friendships have been used for gossiping. Just prior to knowing joy, while having dinner with someone I had just met, I was asked to judge a mutual acquaintance. "Do you think she is a (so-and-so)?" My jaw literally dropped. I was stunned. If I had ever engaged in that kind of conversation before, I did not remember it. For a moment my gut twisted and I stared, not knowing what to say, until something like, "I don't think or speak like that," came out. It would have been more accurate to say that "I *can't* think or speak like that." The conversation must have been very unusual for my dinner companion. Gossiping about or judging people is just not part of my behavior, or my friendships.

For awhile, I challenged my negative mind-reads with a friend. Instead, now I explore ideas, share experiences, engage in light-hearted fun, and give space and presence if a friend is suffering. Any help or reflection that I am asked for will only be provided in a form that helps friends find relief *inside*, if relief is wanted. If I am being asked to help justify feeling bad or to judge someone,

I do not participate. In that case, I concoct and offer all manner of other mind-reads: "Or it could mean this....Or that....What if it meant..." I offer anything else to not support the suffering thought-feelings, until a natural realization sets in that one cannot know for certain and in that, there is the possibility that one need not suffer.

In wondering why people create abusive experiences, or stay in such situations or in uncomfortable friendships, I noticed different tolerance levels. Personally, I have been exposed to a combined physical and verbal violence level of relationships, just the verbal and mental level, and also a loving, peaceful level of co-existence.

I noticed that some people would never accept physical violence, but verbal violence is okay. Some people would never accept verbal violence. Some people accept only love and peace. What I mean by "accept" is not just to say you don't want to be treated like that, or to engage in trying to stop or change someone treating you like that. I mean there is zero tolerance, and that the situation is just left.

When Dad was "being ugly" it usually coincided with drinking, and so we came to blame it on that, which in retrospect actually enabled letting him treat us that way. One day I had had enough, mostly because we had visitors and I felt sorry they were also experiencing this. So I brought this to his attention and told him I did not like it. He said he didn't care. I said I did, and that if he didn't stop, I'd leave.

It was a calm decision I made for myself because I also did not want to be exposed to the abuse, and the idea of leaving felt better than staying, so I was moving toward something better rather than running away from something with fear or anger. I was just looking forward to the peace of happily leaving.

Then the most amazing thing happened. He stopped. He stopped! After all these years of thinking "it was the drinking" and putting up with it, *he stopped*. My relationship with him changed on the spot, and never went back. Apparently, he did care, did want something better, he did love. Yes, he still drank, but his behavior around me was completely different, and we became closer.

By both our actions and our inactions, *we teach people how to treat us*. Once again, we can see how there is no separation. You are as responsible for how someone treats you as they are. Embraced, that is empowering and liberating. It is possible to recognize you are part of it, and to do what you need to do while acting with love for yourself and the other. The rock of love is invincible.

I encourage you to "raise the bar" in your life. Now my preferred level does not even include being in the presence of others bickering together, so often some action is taken. Either something (loving, distracting, or attention redirecting) comes out of my mouth, often changing everything, or I leave.

Interpersonal interactions with people are like dancing, or a reactive game. There is a pattern, and both partners do their part. I noticed a pattern with Dad and I which could be likened to ping-pong. He would "ping" and I would "pong." Well, in order for him to ping back, I would have to pong, and after these events, I began to hate my behavior. I knew it was not me or how I wanted to be or what I wanted to experience. I did not want to pong. So I watched these encounters and saw that there was a gap between ping and pong.

The more I watched, the larger the gap became, until one day there was so much space that there was time to come back with something different. It was so radically different because it came from what I did want, it came from love. The dance was broken because he could not do his part; he could not take the usual step that requires a partner. He could not ping.

You are not separate from others; you are not separate from an interaction; you are not separate from this moment. Once again, our relationship improved and love deepened.

If you have had negative, venting, abusive, or gossipy friends and want to change your habits to foster and experience more peaceful and positive experiences, you may be able to grow with your friends by sharing this intent or changing the dance.

Or, you may grow apart, leaving some relationships and entering into new ones. If that is a conscious decision, be sure to check inside and see it is merely coming from your own bad feeling, fear, hope or judgment, or otherwise clouded perception.

Clear any bad feeling first so you know that your actions are based on clarity and come from love. Love does not mean I will stay with you; love may mean I love both you and me enough to leave this situation.

Beginning to question your bad thought-feelings, and open to intelligence, there's no turning back; you are well on the way to turning lead into gold.

Chapter 24

Key Pointers in Practice

Feel the red flag

When you are in alignment with love and joy, when you are giving and being love and joy, your body feels good. When you are not, you suffer.

Any time you feel a "bad" or "negative" emotion rising, know it is inside, and ask yourself, "What do I want?" and then give it to yourself and look back on the situation. Use suffering to point you toward joy.

At first, your beliefs may only allow you to feel a little better. So it may be just a small feeling of relief. That is okay, that's great. It is a forward feeling shift and experience that has loosened and expanded your beliefs and possibilities. As you practice this, stay with it, and reach for the next best feeling. . .and then the next. . . and the next. See how it grows.

The more you practice this, with big and little things, the more automatic it becomes, and the easier and faster it gets. Soon you will not need the questions. Ultimately, thoughts don't matter anyway—your feeling, your presence of being, does. Soon the shift is done energetically, with just feeling. You will walk in peace and happiness more and more continuously, and your way of being will return to its original truth, that of joy.

{ Do not pollute your beautiful, radiant Being nor the Earth
with negativity. Do not give unhappiness in any form whatsoever
a dwelling place inside you. ~ Eckhart Tolle }

KNOWING WHAT YOU DO WANT

When you ask, "What do I want?" you may get several answers, and quickly. Take the most prominent, most relevant one that feels most like relief, and work with it first. Go back to the others later, if you still need to. If the answer does not come right away or very quickly, that is okay, too; take your time looking.

While you are doing this, it may not feel good, and that is okay because the contrast will help you find it, so stay with it, seeking what feels better. Inside, you will run through things, trying them on, seeing if one feels better, testing if it feels like what you want.

Already you have eased suffering because you are somewhat removed from it; you are looking at it or knowing it as "separate." During this you may need to ask yourself what you want a few times. Then start with whatever comes up; it may just be the opening to more.

STATE WHAT YOU *DO* WANT IN THE POSITIVE

The single habit alone of not answering in the positive could be responsible for much of people's suffering. Usual answers to the first question often go something like this:

I don't want him to speak to me like that because it makes me feel lousy, and then I don't know what to do, so I feel worse, and then it builds and I am afraid I might say something that...

...and on, and on, into the suffering story that *itself* causes suffering in the moment *now*, when he is not even here! Although the habit of mind wants its suffering story to be heard, to be verified, to be supported, to work itself up into a good, unconscious froth, I do not let things go that far. I stop it right at "because…" and ask, "Okay, so what DO you want instead?"

What you want can never be found in what you do not want. Looking at what you don't want can only make you suffer. If you find it challenging to voice what you *do* want, then you may consider making it regular practice at work and home to take five to ten or more minutes each day to keep your attention on what *is* wanted. And in speaking with people, tell them what you do want (not what you don't want). People have a 100% better chance of giving you what you do want *when they know what that is*—instead of their trying to give you what you don't want, which may be the only thing they hear from you.

If what you want is to "feel better," and you are finding that difficult to access, then it may be that you are not being specific enough. Yes, ultimately you want to feel better; however, there is some specific thing you want to experience and the experiencing of that will result in feeling better. Ask yourself this, "You want to feel better; *how?*"

FEELING WHAT YOU WANT

As you begin to answer the second question, "How does it feel?" the first answer may be quick and cerebral; it may be a thought. The real practice begins as you go inside and seek to feel the feeling you want (not just the thought of or label for the feeling).

Remember that feeling is slower than thought; when you first begin to change your feeling, give it time. Look for signs of change: perhaps a release of bodily tension, lowered or raised heart rate, peace, a tingle, a hint of happiness, perhaps a smile beginning to crack. Then when you connect with the desired feeling, notice that good thoughts to support it may follow.

To assist people in tapping into a better feeling in person, I will repeatedly ask, "And what else?" while they go inside. More words may come up, especially as they access the feeling, which is vast and rich. At this point, the three most important things to remember are: (1) take your time to know the feeling, then (2) take some time to enjoy the feeling, (3) appreciate the feeling itself, and then (4) take some more time and enjoy the expanded feeling.

If when feeling for what you do want, you come up with a bad thought-feeling, it may be that you need to work with that first.

For example, someone said:

"If I do this (if I feel good), then I will be afraid of being vulnerable."

Right away I asked how being "afraid of being vulnerable" feels (good or bad?), and if it were bad, I went back to the first question with *it*,

"What do you want instead of being afraid of being vulnerable?"

"To not be afraid of being vulnerable, errrr…to feel safe and secure."

"How does feeling safe and secure feel?"

Typically when done with the secondary issue, I return to the first one, if need be. Sometimes, when reaching for a good feeling, we discover a deeper issue which turns out to be the key one. Or sometimes they are both necessary and I combine them together:

"So, how does doing this and feeling safe and secure, feel?"

Whatever is wanted and needed to move forward toward accessing a better feeling is what is important, and you know this best by checking around inside for what feels like a match that fills the void of the perceived problem and feels like relief, or better. Without a doubt, you will know it when you hit on it.

WHEN TO PRACTICE

Pay attention to how you feel, good or bad, and care about feeling good. If it feels bad, don't accept it—*suspect it!*

Practice every time you notice a "bad" feeling. For some, this red flag will most often be subtle, but more obvious in certain situations. For others, there is a lot of suffering that is "usual" and it may take something more severe to grab the attention. As this practice becomes habitual, you will have fewer, smaller, and more subtle "bad" moments, and more and more joy and enjoyment of life.

If you are struggling to feel better in a situation, then leave the situation temporarily for a few moments; get off the phone, go to the bathroom, or take a walk; anything to take a private break with the intention of using *Alchemy* to give yourself what you want and to know a better feeling before coming back to the situation.

If it was too challenging to do the practice during some situation and you were unable to, then go through the situation in your mind later as soon as you have space, place, and time. Next time you will remember the relief and wisdom you found and have a better chance if such a situation arises again.

While you can't trust the slippery mind, you can rely on the body to let you know when to practice, after all, it is always here and now.

CHAPTER 25

The Body Is Always Here

Practicing all the time, being aware of your body and how you feel and knowing if you are feeling good or bad is actually practicing "being present," or more accurately, presence. Your mind can wander restlessly, but your body is always here, grounded in existence. Practicing awareness is being aware of what is going on in the totality of your reality instead of the limited fraction and fractioning of thought, which you may have noticed replays the same-old, over and over.

Being present stands in stark contrast to having all of your attention channeled into thought; which may be automated, negative, and relentless. The head is the heaviest part of the body; and lost in thought, with all your attention on the stream of thinking around the head, the physical body also becomes unbalanced. If your train of thinking is stressful, your body will also be tense and cramped, and out of alignment.

With your attention placed throughout the body (not just around the head), feeling your feet on the ground, being aware of your breath and opening your peripheral vision, you become grounded. Attention and energy are removed from thought and from perpetuating more thoughts. This is why, when working with people, I will ask them if they are feeling their feet and their breath, and if they are noticing their peripheral vision. Feeling is done with the body, not a thought. When you are present, the mind is available to be used instead of it using you, instead of it keeping your body held captive in stress.

There is calm, stillness, and peace in your presence of being. It is there for you, and others.

Sitting, (called Zazen in Zen), has given me an experiential knowing of what it is like to be lost in thought, and what it is like to wake up from being lost in thought; and also, of complete stillness.

Most people have never sat completely still, physically and mentally. Even while "relaxing," the mind and attention are still moving, the body fidgeting slightly. If all you have ever experienced and known is a constant stream of thinking and movement, how can you know what stillness is like? How can you know how to *be* still? If you have never experienced stillness sitting down, how can you know it when moving about?

This you cannot learn from reading; you must practice some form of sitting still to come to know it. I do not use the term "meditation" because here in the West that has largely come to mean creating some kind of feeling state through listening to music or to an imaginary guided program, which is absolutely not what sitting still is about. As we have seen, the mind has slippery ways to entice you ever so subtly away from this moment. Practicing sitting still calms the monkey mind, taking power and attention away from the sweeping stream of thinking.

While you can use sitting practice for that and many more things, the ultimate use is in waking up: knowing who you really are and finding freedom from the ultimate suffering of birth and death. Whatever your purpose, I highly encourage people to discover what it is to be still through an attained teacher.

There are Zen, Buddhist, and meditative yoga (not merely exercise yoga) teachers, and perhaps others, who can guide you. What is important in whatever tradition or practice you choose is that you learn to be still and aware. Doing that can initially be quite challenging for the beginner because all your life the mind has been busy and you are used to habitually following it with your attention, which wanders. Often the breath is used as a touchstone to help stabilize attention.

{ The mind is the king of the senses, and the breath
is the king of the mind. ~ BKS Iyengar }

Being still no matter what, including not itching, and not allowing the body to wander with the mind, was at first very challenging for me, like it is for most people. You feel an itch, and the mind says you must scratch, but you come to know it is the mind that is itching. The more you scratch, the more you itch.

The mind may make a scene trying to convince you that you can't be still, and your teacher will help you burn through this. For a while I experienced the common all over body "itch" but eventually, the body and breath settled the mind down and now that no longer happens. So you may go through this, like others. Knowing that it's the same for all, and that it will end, helps you to sit through even itchy thoughts like "I can't do this,"—and you can come to know you are not a thought, that you are before and beyond thoughts, and you can know freedom from the habitual thinking dictatorship, in your actual life.

I have known several people who said they tried sitting still and "just couldn't do it, it just wasn't for them," and I can attest that I used to think that way too, but now I know it wasn't me speaking. That was the sense of a separate me, the "ego," which wants its way. In their case the monkey mind dictator won. In mine, I sat right through noticing those thoughts. Then the monkey mind gave up, and the itch, the unreal itch which kept tempting me here…and then there… and then over here, stopped.

It was well worth it, beyond what I could describe in a book. Don't let some little negative thought-feeling get in the way of making some of the greatest discoveries of your life. It is the same negative habit pattern that has been running, and perhaps ruining, your life.

Learning to sit still is also an opportunity to learn to value what is, to come to know what your life is and to appreciate the life that breathes you more than the transient content of your life.

It is an opportunity to get re-acquainted with the miracle of this and every moment. Learning to sit still will also help you excel in coming to your senses when using *Alchemy* (and vice versa because they both use awareness and attention).

When you combine your powers of presence and attention you can start to see everything as it is, with love. Then a gratitude that brings its own reward fills you. After some time I was surprised yet again to discover what living in joy is *really* like.

CHAPTER 26

Equanimity

WHAT LIVING IN JOY IS LIKE

Feeling good has become predominant for me and positive, peaceful thoughts flow freely alongside. The difference between now and when I had the three days of bliss that faded back to the "usual" is that now I know how joy "happens" and I can re-establish it, moment to moment. I do this so habitually that happiness and joy have become my near-constant companions, with suffering being a short-lived indicator of what I want.

A friend once asked me if I missed someone. The answer was no, because "missing" now means that I want to feel them, so I get to have that. When I want someone who is not present, I now know how to "experience them." There is never any feeling of missing.

Everywhere I go there is so much to enjoy and celebrate! What joy in feeling and offering love and appreciation to all that is seen! Just walking through the neighborhood, the sheer magic and wonder of a majestic, living, breathing tree fills me with reverence and awe. Even the garbage floating around triggers good thoughts and feeling: there is work and livelihood for someone, there is something we created that did some good, it was enjoyed, and the sheer existence and brilliance of vibrant colors, sounds, breezes—the miracle of experience itself. Simply the sensations of the breath are pleasurable.

For about eight months that is how life was for me, but then something unexpected happened. When you know you can have whatever feeling and experience you want, then your energy and attention are not consumed with feeling good or not feeling bad. When you are not obsessed with how you feel, you are not attached to feeling good or bad, and even if some negative feeling arises, it does not last long, and it cannot stay because there is no fear of it, there is no attachment. You can get on with living, or investigating life more deeply.

Now I simply notice and ignore negative thoughts or states, and without my attention, they fade away. When you stop feeding the birds, they stop coming.

An enormous amount of time and energy is released and becomes available when you are no longer seeking or avoiding some thing outside you. Seeking, wanting, and needing can get you in trouble; in work trouble, in financial trouble, and in relationship trouble.

Instead, you stop looking outside, have more and more love and happiness *spontaneously* inside, and oddly, *the outside and inside don't matter*, and they stop appearing different or separate. You become available to so much more productivity, value and purpose, and you thrive in that. A sense of wholeness and peace settles in deeper and deeper. Knowing and living love and joy is really living in equanimity and freedom.

What matters most when living in lack or pain is seeking joy. What mattered most for me after actualizing joy was knowing the eternal Divine, because in the end, even "good" experiences are impermanent. That shift in attention and inquiry did not go unanswered.

To actualize freedom and to free energy, you must deeply realize that you are the source of all you seek and that you are always with yourself, so there is nothing you will *ever* need.

CHAPTER 27

Don't Just Fill Your Cup
—Realize It Is Bottomless

After an *Alchemy* session, people leave feeling happy and peaceful. One day a client called to make an appointment, "I really need it," she said.

That, along with some other readers' comments like, "I read your book when I need a tune-up," and, "It picks me up when I feel down," brought to my attention the need for more emphasis on using the practice to realize your innate freedom, your bottomless cup—permanently, through the destruction of even these old beliefs.

To know the freedom that you are once and for all, your intention for doing the practice must be to use suffering to break through to freedom. Instead of believing bad thought-feelings, *notice that they are just thoughts* right now where you are, wherever you are. You don't need this book. That is an outside thing. You don't need me. You don't need a session to "tune up," to "recharge your battery," or to "fill your cup" or your "tank." Break through even *those* attachment thoughts—which cannot feel good or pure and free. Use the practice with them.

When you truly realize that nothing outside of you can make you feel good, and that nothing outside of you can make you feel bad, and that you can enjoy this life that is living you at any time, no matter what is going on outside; then you know true freedom and peace of mind that does not waiver.

Your life, your experience, may change fundamentally in these ways (or more) like mine did:

- You know that no thing, no person, no event can emotionally hurt you.
- Weather does not affect you negatively.
- You need nothing and no one; you are self-fulfilling.
- Nothing stresses you; there is nothing you hate doing.
- You are so self-fulfilled that you have more to give than take; you love without condition.
- You are comfortable everywhere.
- You may see old-mind rising and laugh at it as an option.
- Nothing is serious, because you have freedom of experience; life becomes lighter.
- You may find yourself challenged with habitual speech for a while, modifying it to better reflect truth.
- You may see unconsciousness or suffering in others, and relate with compassion.
- You may engage in the experience of so much love, connection, joy, and peace that it becomes bliss or ecstasy.
- You sense non-separation from all that eternally is.
- You may burst out laughing (or crying with love) at times.
- You love yourself, all beings great and small, and all creation.
- Emotional charge from negative thought ceases.
- You are fearless and free.
- There is a deep sense of peace and well-being.

To others, these changes are invisible, but the internal change is undeniable. You do not see the outside the same way anymore. No one else knows what has happened, no one else "gets it" like you do. Initially what goes on around you does not change (although people may seem to have changed because your perspective has), and since you stop reacting the way you used to, over time relationships may change.

What has kept those people who come for "refills" from knowing their infinite freedom? There they are, feeling bad, and saying they need a fill-up instead of noticing the bad feeling and using the practice with it.

Some people use *Alchemy* once or twice and then stop because they have not instantly arrived where expected or desired. Using how you feel as a navigation system is much like piloting a plane. Did you know that on its flight an airplane is mostly "off course?"

First of all, planes fly fairly straight but the earth is round, and then there is weather (good and bad), birds, national security, mechanical challenges, and other planes or airborne objects that periodically put it off course. It does have a course heading, but it is constantly monitoring and perpetually correcting course using its guidance system.

If anywhere on the trip the plane felt one strong wind that pushed them off course and then thought (and believed), "Ah well that's it, it did not work. I quit," then it would *never* arrive. Using *Alchemy* is much like that, especially at first. We have a sophisticated guidance system, and it's called feeling. Feeling bad is not an indicator of failure, it is a directional instrument that points the way. So while doing this, accept no bad thought, no bad feeling and do not stop. Use whatever arises and just keep going and moving in the right direction.

Or perhaps people have stopped because of the deep-seated fundamental belief that the outside magically controls how we feel. Some will parrot the thought, "Only I can hurt myself." Ask the same person if they can feel good if their bank account is empty, a lover leaves, or a friend dies, and the answer will likely be, "Oh…well, no. "

Some people say, "No one can hurt me unless I 'all How, specifically, do you do this allowing? Pain is felt phy in your body-mind during the contraction of suffering. How someone else do this contracting for you? How do you "all them to do this contracting for you, inside?

Remember that concepts can be anything, and need no dire connection to reality. Without looking into the reality of the words without looking into truth, we suffer due to this unconsciousness.

Offered to recognize a bottomless cup instead of a refill, the client responded, "You mean you can feel good even if your daughter says she never wants to see you again?"

"Yes," I replied.

"You mean even if your partner dies…and if.…and if…?"

"Yes. Yes. Yes."

With good feeling comes access to more information and more possibilities. As we all have seen or will see, one day when your partner or daughter is still not present in body, suddenly you will feel good. One day your estranged daughter may change her mind. Mind is fickle and in a blind rage the words "never" may be uttered and then later, with better feeling and clarity, regretted (or forgotten). Maybe right now, with your daughter's behavior, *you* really don't want her in your presence at this time. And the thing is, *we don't know the future.* We don't know if a daughter will never come back or if she will—*the daughter does not even know.*

When you truly see someone's attack as a cry for help, you feel compassion, not hurt. But you can't know that while feeling attacked. When you know someone you love hurts to be around you, then for *whatever* their reason or belief, in true love you will not want them to be around you.

Love does not cling, love does not need. Love is space. And just maybe space is good for them and you for a while. And maybe never seeing you in this lifetime *is* good. How can we know what is best for another? Or even ourselves? We don't know the future and so the only way to know is by what is now. What is—is—and it is always changing. There is never a "forever" with any outside experience. Yet, ultimately, the feeling of your daughter is within you and can never be taken away.

You can use *Alchemy* to feel a bit better in the moment (and have to keep coming back for a "refill"), or you can use it to realize some truth of your inherent freedom.

YOU ARE THE SOURCE

When you suffer, you are the source of the feeling. When you feel good with a lover—or without—you are the source of the feeling. We have confused people for feeling. We have confused things for feeling. We have confused events for feeling. Feeling comes from appying and believing thoughts, meaning, via your powers of attention and interest, which are independent of every thing. They are body-mind functions, like breathing, of which you can take conscious control.

Once you have experienced this, mind may continue to say otherwise—saying it's not real or not right, or you can;'t have that, but shine your light of awareness, consciousness, attention, and presence on the good feeling anyway, whihc counters with: "But it IS!" and choose, prefer, and sustain attention there, with what is.

Accept the good feeling, by enjoying it. Nurture it. The "rightness" of it will become apparent with the intelligence that comes with the expansion of feeling good. Eventually old-mind will erode and fade into the other option it always was.

As the source, you can then realize that you don't need anything, but that does not mean that you will go without anything; to the contrary you *gain* everything. You will become invulnerable through total vulnerability and exposure to what is, and experiencing that you are okay, regardless. Then bravery becomes a joke because you learn there was never anything to be afraid of in the beginning.

HOW DO YOU HAVE THIS ALCHEMICAL BREAKTHROUGH?

Begin to "play" with feeling—even good feeling; and you'll find you can even enhance feeling through attention, enjoyment, and appreciation. Whatever you thought the source was, as soon as you notice a feeling, feel into the body and take conscious ownership.

Decide and intend to use this practice to experience and realize freedom. Recognize *any* and *every* bad thought-feeling and reject them all (by not believing them, not entertaining them, ignoring them, and by seeking and keeping your interest and attention on a better feeling). Use the "joy" in the *Alchemy of Love and Joy*™ and set feeling good now as your highest priority, and use the love in *Alchemy*, to be determined not to blame any person or outside "cause" for your pain. You are the power, so do not accept any bad thought-feeling, as you seek only a better one, inside.

Feel fantastic in the face of adversity, and you could break the inherited suffering of generations, and nothing outside can ever hurt you again, because you will know that they never did. Recognize, practice, and live as the bottomless cup that you are.

THERE IS NO ARRIVAL, THERE IS NO FAILURE

It is said that Thomas Edison failed one thousand times when trying to invent the light bulb. When asked about it, he said he did not fail; he just found one thousand ways *not* to make a light bulb. In NLP we have a similar saying, "There is no failure; there is only feedback."

Children learning to walk fall down many times, but they do not stay down, they push off the ground and stand again, over and over. What if they told themselves, "Forget it, it's not possible!"? Become child-like, because innocence, freedom from thought—*not knowing*, is where all possibilities lie.

{ If you think you can do a thing or think you can't
do a thing, you're right. ~ Henry Ford }

{ Those that say it can't be done should get out of the way of those
doing it. ~ Chinese Proverb }

When you "fall" down, don't sit there and proclaim failure or inability, nor believe any other bad thought-feeling. Reject them all, because *they* are suffering. Use the ground of presence, of awareness, to push off again. If you are not feeling good in one moment, it is not because there is something fundamentally or fixedly wrong with you, like the conceptual idea that your "cup is empty" and needs an (outside) refill. If you are not feeling good in this moment, *it is time to*—and in the next moment, and the next, until you are.

This alchemical practice is something you do, moment to moment, every moment. There is no way to do it wrong, and there is no "arrival" point where you are done with doing this.

The first critical breakthrough is one you already have and will always have; *you know you can always answer the questions.* Then you will know that bad feeling can never stay, and that you don't need to believe suffering.

Then one day you will notice seeking joy is your primary habit, just like the habitual suffering was. Then another day it will become subtle and automatic, and you may even notice that you no longer use the questions. You may notice suffering thoughts less and less, and then finally feeling good or not feeling bad no longer matters, and equanimity and peace settle in.

THE PURPOSE OF THE PRACTICE

The purpose of the practice is to know freedom, not permanent happiness (as we have known it). People ask me if my state is always one of joy. When I first learned I could "cause" joy, I was like a kid who discovered they were in a candy store, and that all the candy was free. I pigged out! I went around in a happy, energized state for about six weeks, until I realized that the body also needed something else; it wasn't experiencing other positive, rejuvenating states like rest, relaxation, and peace.

So now I am like a kid in a free candy store with unlimited variety. Do not seek some "arrival state" where you are always and only happy. Joy is a tool. The purpose of the practice is to realize freedom so that you can reside in a wholesome state, no matter what mind throws at you—or if sadness or some other negative state does arise, then you are not attached to it, you know it is not you, and that it cannot stay.

Watching the turmoil on the surface of the ocean, deep within you are still and can watch the waves, allowing them to play and pass by, as you know they always do.

Once you realize your freedom, automatic negative thoughts cease to have any power, and there is an underlying base sense of peace and empowerment.

The knowledge that there is no arrival is good news indeed; that means there is also no failure, and no "exit" or end to joy, peace, love, bliss, and ecstasy. Your cup can't be empty, and it can't be full...because it is bottomless.

{ Nobody has ever measured, not even poets,
how much the heart can hold. ~ Zelda Fitzgerald }

But do you want it? You must *desire* it, and not as in feeling bad because you don't have it (which is a movement away from it), but the pull of love towards it. With this desire lit, you will find your purpose and intention; your last conceptual boat to the other shore.

CHAPTER 28

Simple Examples

The following are true examples of people who have shifted their internal experience and their external (behavioral) ones by using *The Alchemy of Love and Joy*™.

These examples may seem short, and the process sometimes is, however, each went deeply into the feeling they wanted, and time and space (that aren't visible here) allowed for that. Sometimes all the shifts and realizations that come are not verbalized in coherent words. This is an energetic, feeling practice, and words are not necessary for change.

ANXIOUS FOR DAUGHTER

What do you want?
  "I want my daughter to not be anxious. I want her to be peaceful."
How does your daughter feeling peace, feel?
  "It feels <closing eyes>…calm, relaxed. Light. Happy."
Is this how you prefer to feel?
  <relaxed grin> "Definitely."
Feeling this way, how do you act?
  "Oh, much more beneficial for her. I am strong, and there for her. My peaceful presence helps her much more!"
Is this what you prefer to give and send her?
"Absolutely!"

I MISS MY EX-GIRLFRIEND

What do you want?

"To feel connected to her."

How does feeling connected to her feel?

<closing eyes> "It feels…connected, close, warm…soothing, relaxing. Seeing her, feeling her closeness, I feel good about me, about her, about us. Everything is okay. Everything is very, very good."<smiling, relaxing>

Is that what you prefer to feel?

<eyes open wide> "Oh yes, definitely. It feels fantastic. Wow! I can feel this good even without her…haha!" "Yes, it feels so much better…not just a relief, it feels really, really good to feel that connection."

Feeling this way, how do you act?

<eyes closed, processes silently inside, nods>

"Oh! Okay, I get it."

Is that what you prefer to project?

"Well, yes, if she does receive energy, I do care, and this is certainly what I'd rather send. And certainly if we do end up in the same room, this would be a better feeling."

DECEASED PARENTS

What do you want?

"I want to be close to my parents."

How does being close to them feel?

"It feels <closing eyes, head turning-up>…warm. Safe. <body relaxes> Good. And comforting. Supported. Like they are there for me. It feels like…Wow…Ohhh.. it feels like…I am them…and they are me. I am them, and they are me…<pleasant, ethereal smile>."

Is this how you prefer to feel?

　　<relaxed grin> "Definitely."

Feeling this way, how do you act?

　　"More calm, confident. Supported....I get things I want done. In control."

Is this what you prefer to do, and to send them?

　　"Oh yes!!"

CHAPTER 29

Case Example 1

"This Won't Be Easy."

"This sounds good, but....feeling is hard."

How does that feel?

"It feels like this won't be easy."

How does that feel, good? Or bad?

"Oh, <pause> bad."

What do you want instead?

"I want to be free."

OK, let's back up and take one at a time... you said "It won't be easy,"
right?

"Yes."

And that feels bad, or not good, right?

"Right."

So use any thing, any thought, every thought and moment that does not feel
good, and...

What do you want instead, specifically?

"Uhm, oh I guess for it to be easy."

Okay, and how does it being easy feel?

"Good."

Are you feeling your feet on the ground? Your breath?
Seeing your peripheral vision?

"What is that about?" <listener asks>

<Cindy addresses room> *When I first ask the question "How does it feel?" the response is usually fast and cerebral; it is about thinking, not feeling. Feeling is done with the body, not the head, not with a thought. The question is cerebral, but the answer needs to be done bodily. This is how I get people to feel into their body as they search for the answer. They answer from the body, from feeling. You notice their body language changes, and the thought and speech slow down. Remember, the body feels and is slower than thought. Our intention here is not to know the answer, but to feel it.*

So, feeling into your body, your breath, and opening your vision, how does this "being easy" feel?

"Well…it feels light…" <smiles>

Good. How else?

"Happy, and very light… like I am walking two feet off the ground."

Wow, fun… is this what you prefer to feel?

"Yes."

And as you are feeling light and two feet off the ground, how do you act?

"Well, I am more positive!" <grins><audience laughs>

Notes:

The participant had not done *Alchemy* yet, and so could not even know how easy it can be. Based on unproven, unsupported thoughts, the thought, "It won't be easy," surfaced and was believed. The irony: it is the state caused by this unproven thought itself that could make it "not easy." When you clear the negative state, the negative thought not only dissolves—it is replaced by its opposite.

CHAPTER 30

Case Example 2

"Why Do I Feel So *Bad*?"

You hurt because you hurt. Reasons will not end it. To the contrary, reasons support it. This illustrates how looking for reasons for your pain only perpetuates the pain, and is a demonstration of how, using Alchemy, you can know the good feeling and peace which were always already the case (and so are always available).

A conversation, also in video on the website:
http://www.AlchemyLoveJoy.com

Cindy has invited the participant to come up a few times to work with her…

<distraught, crying> "But will they (thoughts) go away for good?"
I know…
  "I've got such much to be thankful for Cindy."
Yes!
  "…So much!…why do I feel so shitty?"
<Cindy motions and invites her up>…*Come up?*
    <participant gets up>
Yah <clapping>
The whys are coming up, I know. And they try their hardest, don't they?

"I ask my doctor that…'Why?' And she said it's your mind. Your mind's getting in there."

You don't need a why. Do you?

<shakes head>

"I keep searching for why though. I want to know why."

Why? Why the search for a why? Have you ever found it in a why?

<shakes head>

"No."

You're not going to find it in a why.

<shakes head>

You know that.

<nods head>

So. Is there a good reason to keep a why?

<shakes head>

"No."

"The pain…"

What do you want instead?

<crying>: "I want the pain to go away. There is so much…so much to be grateful for…"

Yes.

"So much good stuff and I can't enjoy it… I'm so stuck and I…I just hate it. I pick myself up and I brush myself off, and I get right back down again. It's like.…You were talking about that incident with work…I didn't just stay home for the day, I quit the job. So I could get away from them because they were hurting me. But its not about them hurting me, it's me. I know that. I still can't get rid of it. <shaking head> I know that."

Yes. And knowing that is not something to beat yourself up with, okay. Knowing that is a tool. Okay?

<nods head>

You know. You are so close. You're so close. This is good.

<nods head>

So can you think of a time, a particular time…I don't want you to go into it…I want you to stay here with me, okay? Feel your feet on the chair, the floor, okay?

<nods head>

Can you think of a time when that arose, a particular time…You were feeling okay, and then out of the blue…? Do you have a particular time, place where you were…?

You had one here earlier, didn't you? A time when you were feeling okay, and then, a thought arose…whatever it was, and you started to feel bad. You noticed a bad feeling. So you were feeling okay, and then you noticed a bad feeling. Can you remember a time where you were when that happened?

"It's that same incident…at work."

Okay. One particular incident, okay, gonna use that one at work?

"It's the workers, but yeah."

<Cindy addresses audience>: *So, you don't even actually have to go into the content when you're working with me…usually, because you do it all inside, so I don't need to know the details. If you want to share that's okay, but you don't have to.*

So, as long as you have the situation. Okay, yes. In that moment when you noticed the bad feeling, what did you want? What specifically did you want?

"To be accepted." <voice cracks>

To be accepted…very good, okay. Now at this point it's very critical because mind's habit will try to flip you into the opposite…okay? To be "not accepted," okay? Your job here is to keep your attention on being accepted. Good. Yah. Good. Okay?

So, in that moment…how does feeling accepted feel? You do know how it feels, right?

<nods head>

<Cindy addresses room>: *Yes. Everyone here has felt not accepted before, right?…And you felt accepted, so you do know what that's like. Very good…yes, you do. So how does feeling accepted feel?*

"Embracing, comforting."

Yes.

"Comforting."

Comforting. Yeah. Feel the embrace. Yeah. How else does it feel?

"Loved and cared for. Gentle."

Gentle. Loved, cared for, gentle. Warm, Embracing. Okay.

I want you to ask yourself and answer it with your body, okay? Look for it in your body and tell me when you have it. How does feeling accepted and warm and embraced feel? Good. Got it, eh? Good. Okay. Keep your attention on that, because it feels good right? Okay. Enjoy it. Good. Nice. That's right.

<starts crying>

No, stay with it…

Cindy <addresses room>: *See what happened? In that moment, she felt it, I don't know if you guys were watching…she relaxed, she felt it…and then what happened?*

Then something happened, right? What happened?

"I won't allow it…I pushed it back…"

This is why it's very important to continue practicing allowing it. It's one thing I'd highly suggest you do at home, is practice this. Go, stop, in the middle of the day for no reason, go to the same place and sit and get cozy. Snuggle into something warm and start to feel how accepted feels and enjoy it. Some thought may come up, and I'd like to do some work with you, maybe later because we can go really deeply. There is perhaps something in there that's coming up… and it happens so fast…and the habit is to buy into it and believe it and so your attention goes off. So practice as much as you can, sustaining this feeling. Okay? I want you to try it again, look for that in your body. Answer it with your body, and keep your attention there.

<nods head>

How does feeling accepted feel?

<participant breathes deeply and sighs>

<participant laughs, Cindy laughs>

Yah, yah.

Sustain it. Sustain it. Just sustain it right there. Don't take it any further. Just enjoy that amount right there. Yeah. Good. Are you feeling your feet on the floor? You hear the clock? Yeah? Okay. Is this how you prefer to feel? Yes. Stay with it. Good. That's right.

Okay, it dropped didn't it? So ask again: How does acceptance feel? And let your body answer.

<Participant breathes deeply and sighs, relaxes.>

Is this how you prefer to feel? Sustain. Because you want it, right?

<laughter>

So hold it. Enjoy that, appreciate it. Yes. Let it to grow. To whatever it will grow…Nice. Very good. Sustain it. Good. Enjoying that and sustaining it, [laughter] good, notice the thought, that may come up, that whatever it was, I don't know what it was, that says "oh you can't feel that way"

<laughter>…

Well done..

You noticed that thought, huh? What do you think of it now?"

<Participant bursts out laughing.>

<Participant laughs, puts hand over mouth in shock, shaking head.>

<laughter>

Powerful, huh?

"I can have this anytime I want…"

Anytime you want. Wherever you are. How much gratitude is in that, huh?

"I've been searching all my life for it…45 years."

It's been here.

Notes:

Tentative and afraid of more pain, the participant wanted assurance before coming up and asked "But will they (bad thoughts) go away for good?" No. Nor should they, however, you can be done with believing in bad thoughts and experiencing suffering. Thoughts are not inherently bad. You can notice them and they don't matter, as she discovers.

Chapter 31

Case Example 3—Judgment

"He's a Fake!"

An actual conversation.

"He's a fake"
What do you want?
"I want him to have authenticity and depth."
How does him having authenticity and depth, feel?
<pauses, winces> "I feel pain suddenly."
Emotional or physical?
"Physical. I find it's not easy to feel authenticity and depth."
Okay, you find it's not easy, what do you want instead?
"I want…it to be easy to feel authenticity and depth."
Okay, so how does easy to feel authenticity and depth, feel?
"Light and sunny."
Good, enjoy that feeling…
"Oh…the pain's gone."
Very good, and feeling light and sunny, how does authenticity and depth feel?
"It feels….genuine, trustworthy."
That's right, enjoy that….Now take that light, sunny, genuine, and trustworthy feeling and appreciate it…
<body shifts, straightens>
What just happened?
"It grew."

Wonderful, just enjoy that now. And feeling this way, think of him.

"I…I can't." <incredulous look>

Oh? Huh. Well, you know his behavior, right? (My mind-read here was that it was his behavior that was perceived as fake.)

"Yes, but I can't get him back."

Then what you can't get back is your judgment of him, and that feeling. See his behavior at the same time as you feel the authenticity, depth, and trust. Like reprimanding children, we don't say they are bad, we say the behavior is bad, because people are not their behavior.

"Yes, right."

So you can see the behavior and just leave it be without giving it negative meaning. There are perhaps twenty or thirty possible meanings. We apply the meaning (to others, to the outside) that we are missing inside, that we are denying ourselves. When you give yourself what you stopped giving yourself, in this case trust and being your true authentic self, you cannot judge, you cannot feel judgment.

Is this what you prefer to feel?

"Yes."

Is this your true authentic self?

"Yes."

Then who was really faking?

"Ohhh…"<processing>

Notes:

My mind-read with this participant was that it was something about his behavior that was fake, when in fact I later discovered it was the way he dressed. No wonder she could no longer see him!

When we judge people, we no longer see the real, or whole, person—all we can know is our label and the associated feeling. If you are not accessing that bad feeling, then you can't even see the label that replaced the person. And what, in our reality, is left of the person? Nothing. Well, that is a step better than seeing the person as a label. It also makes space for more of the truth to be known, because as we know, no one person is one thought (like a judgment is).

In this moment this participant did not feel genuine on the inside, and so could not see it on the outside. Perception is projection. The world is your mirror. If you don't have or feel something inside, then you can't have or see it outside.

With judgment, when we "point a finger" at someone, we are pointing at ourselves, and when we turn the judgment around (e.g., "I am a fake") the truth of the mirror can be seen. Explore turning your judgment around as many ways as possible, and you can see how the opposite can, as Byron Katie says, be "as true, or truer." (e.g., "He is not a fake." After all, he genuinely was wearing the clothes he wears, not yours, or someone else's.)

CHAPTER 32

Why Do People Die By Suicide?

CONSIDERING SUICIDE?

If you have considered or are considering suicide, let me ask you this: If you broke an arm would you just keep using it normally, or would you use the pain as a signal to get treatment? The brain is an organ, and like other body parts, it can have a physical problem that needs care, and mental pain is the signal to get help. If you are struggling, please call one of the emergency lines at the beginning of this book. There is much love and support to get you through, and this state *will* change, because as you know, everything changes.

A SOCIAL PROBLEM

Some people's life situations presented an immense struggle to "measure up" to what is valued in society, and who could not. Some people carried a secret that was unbearable to them. Some people were tortured by bad thought-feelings they believed. Some people experienced such severe and painful depression for unknown reasons that death seemed the only option, the only release. Some people experienced a combination of the above.

Some people had everything that society says is important: the career, the lover, the home, the money, the family, and the friends, and society cannot understand at all why they died by suicide. If you cannot understand that, then perhaps you yourself believe that these worldly possessions are "where it's at." But you can have everything on the outside and experience a complete void on the inside because once again, *we don't want things, people, or events.*

What pushed me to look for something more was frustration with the void created by all the false thoughts that we are given to believe in, which never satisfy. Those thoughts cannot be fully believed in because reality and truth keep rattling them. Not many people face this, even fewer openly, and so there may be no one to talk to about it and one can feel alone and hopeless.

The confusion about who we are with thoughts is rampant in society. I would hold it very likely that most, if not all, the people who died by suicide did not know they were not thoughts, and/or could not separate themselves from thought; could not stop fueling the stream of stressful thinking. When you believe a thought is true, or real, or important, you bring it to life in your experience, you feel worse, have more and worse thoughts, feel worse--and in this way you can spiral downward, depressing the body-mind.

In addition being confused about ourselves, the false joy presented by this materialistic, consumer-oriented society must be held accountable as having contributed to some suicides. I saw this false message most blatantly one Christmas season, in the largest sign I have ever seen, that screamed: *Bigger Toy, Bigger Joy!* It belonged to a car dealership.

So those unable to buy a new car are relegated to lesser joy, right? Wrong. But deeply conditioned people may believe this; they may believe that they need bigger toys and therefore they may experience lesser joy, or even anxiety or depression, without them, especially without being able to provide them for loved ones. They may suffer, they may steal, they may overeat, they may go into debt, they may do drugs, they may do harm, and they may die by suicide.

Suicide may be an outcome of the ultimate confusion of things, people, or events, with feeling and pain; people may confuse ending their pain with ending their life. But these are two different things. You don't know whether ending this life will end the pain, but we do know the pain can be stopped in this body.

You have seen how the average person's judgment and access to truth can be clouded. Judgment, reality, and truth are never more clouded than when experiencing so much pain that someone considers ending their life. After too much pain for too long, or for other reasons, the brain can acquire a chemical imbalance that can additionally cloud thinking. It's not that someone is weak.

I've worked with people who have suicidal ideation, and every one of them says it's not that they want to die, they just want the pain to stop and can't see any other way out.

It is said that suicide happens when pain exceeds the resources (inner and outer) available to cope with the pain. Isolation, due to the subject of suicide being taboo, with painful stigma attached, exacerbates the problem. Someone at this point who is also isolated and is unable to talk about suicidal thoughts has run out of resources. We as a society need to educate the public to allieviate the fear of speaking about suicide, so we can have open dialogue, and keep this resource available at this critical junction.

When people talk about being alone, a burden, having no purpose, being hopeless, having no escape, or when they withdraw from life, consider these as "invitations" to talk about suicide. For many reasons, the person suffering cannot bring the subject up themselves, so please ask if they are considering harming themselves.

Take heart! "Talking is proof of living," I say, so do not be afraid to bring up the subject of suicide with someone you think is struggling. It will not "give them the idea," if they didn't already have it, nor cause suicide, but it may become their last resource if they already are thinking about suicide. You can get more resources and read more about how to help someone with suicidal ideation on my website: http://alchemylovejoy.com.

MARKETING MANIPULATES THE MASSES, FEEDS UNCONSCIOUSNESS

There is nothing wrong with having material things, but confusing them with happiness results in suffering. Marketing purposely uses people's attachments, fears, and hopes, and the mass unconscious, to drive people to buy. With messages that claim the source of joy is in some thing, person, or event, they continually feed this belief with a sense of lack, and spread the idea that we need outside things—and that *imagined* need *is inexhaustible, inextinguishable,* and *unquenchable.* It is an addiction.

When the masses discover the truth that *inexhaustible, inextinguishable* and *completely quenching* joy is within them and only within them, then current marketing tactics will lose power and will have to evolve. In that way, we have the power to change marketing strategies that contribute to unconsciousness, and the conditioning and suffering of future generations.

THE BIG QUESTIONS NO ONE ASKS

Beyond sensing that the material world does not quench, a subtle, yet persistent, knowing voice inside calls you to discover something more—something much more. And you may wonder...

Where did I come from? What am I doing here? What happens when I leave? Where do I go? When we did ask these questions that no one dares ask, maybe as a child, perhaps we were told not to ask those questions, or that they were stupid questions, or that nobody knew the answer.

Eventually, children quit asking. Perhaps they do not want to feel bad, or perhaps they figure out that adults don't know. For me it was both.

No one who has not realized their true Self knows the answers to the big questions, because the questions are based on a limited, separated, false idea of themselves. What is necessary is dropping the false beliefs from which the questions arise, so the truth can be revealed. This book begins to question the assumptions about happiness and suffering, beginning to unravel the knots and make space for truth and peace to be known. That is a fine starting place, but don't stop there.

CHAPTER 33

Reality Rattles Beliefs

—resulting in dissatisfaction

You may be coming to the same conclusion I have, that beliefs are a major source of much of our suffering. The good news is that beliefs are just thoughts.

Repeated thoughts, associated with either good or bad feeling, with an added feeling of conviction, can become "beliefs." Repeated thoughts become familiar, and familiarity is associated with "real." What we think is real, we believe, we live, we create—and we experience.

Repeated negative thoughts can become your familiar "comfort" zone. Through that familiarity we can create a negative "truth" and negative experience of our reality, like "The world is full of bad people, the world is a nasty place"—but it's only a generalized thought, after another thought, after another thought.

And as you know, the world cannot be a thought. Because thoughts and beliefs can be deleted, distorted, and generalized, they do not match reality, which itself cannot be deleted, distorted, or generalized. So reality is your friend, always bumping up against you and rattling your beliefs, always pointing you to what is real and true and safe, because reality does not cause psychological suffering.

Beliefs also represent the past. They are formed on it, and also on an anticipation of the future. It is all very limiting. Without ideas of the future, the future is free to be more than you can think or imagine. When your sense of identity no longer comes from the past or the future, then it comes directly out of presence, directly out of awareness, out of the unlimited now.

Until you are non-attached, you hold beliefs; some conscious and obvious, others normally operating under your level of awareness. Some beliefs are resourceful to a limited degree, for a while, and some are damaging. Suffering is the surfacing of a bad thought belief—and an opportunity to see the belief.

What had a major effect on the freedom and peace in my life was the dropping away of beliefs, and even of the belief in beliefs. Since even a "good" belief is a limit, what if we held no beliefs? As we have seen, (1) beliefs are just thoughts and as such, they are not necessary to living your life and (2) the majority of our thoughts have no value whatsoever, and many of them are actually negative and damaging.

Just for a moment, toss all beliefs aside and see what happens. Just be there, feeling completely into your body, without a single thought or belief for just a moment.

~

Notice your heart keeps beating. Do you really need a belief in order to be here, to breathe, or in order to take care of your life? Life goes on quite fine, thank you, without any beliefs at all. Do this for half a day. Then a day. Then a week. Then see…

PS—This includes tossing religious beliefs, if for just a moment. Notice that Source, the Divine, the Universe, God, the All that Is…does not need your belief, nor your non-belief. Can you let the All that Is, God, the Universe, the Divine, or Source be bigger than your thoughts?

Knowing, which is wordless and before thought, and which you cannot lose or toss, is already the case, and it needs no beliefs or thoughts. Action, not thought, is necessary. Non-attached, belief-free action is wise, holistic action. *But don't believe me.*

CHAPTER 34

Don't Believe Anything

—and that includes what I say

A belief is a dead end. It is a passive acceptance, a stopping point. I can't give you my realization, my actualization, my knowing, in any way, and that includes through words in a book. You must come to your own by not stopping by believing, but instead by stepping into something new, trying it on, and seeing, knowing, touching, tasting, feeling, hearing what is true for you in your experience.

That action is what makes realization of something, "realization." It makes it more than a concept, more than a thought, more than an unlived, simply spoken belief. It *actualizes* it. Thoughts are not experience. Thoughts are not direct Knowing.

{ Do not quench the Spirit. Do not despise prophetic utterances.
Test everything; retain what is good.
~ New Testament, 1 Thess. 5:19–21 }

{ Believe nothing, no matter where you read it, or who said it,
no matter if I have said it, unless it agrees with your own reason
and your own common sense.
~ Siddhartha Gautama (The Buddha), 563–483 B.C. }

Perhaps the Buddha and other great sages have said not to believe them not only so that they would not be put on a pedestal, out of reach, iconized, made into something non-human, above-human, or unreachable, but even more importantly, so that we would not hit the dead end of a belief and settle on a thought *about* something; so that we would *do* what we need to do, like they did, to attain what we will attain.

It is only through the acts of questioning, doubting, testing, and trying on that you can discover—discover what you did not know before. This can only be done through questioning your assumptions and beliefs, viewing them face to face with your direct experience. If these conflict, the old beliefs and assumptions will erode and be replaced with your own clear, true knowing.

Don't stop at a bad feeling. Don't stop at a good feeling. Even a "good" belief is a limitation. Don't believe, don't disbelieve. It's better to be not knowing because in that there is infinite space. Question everything, whole-heartedly, whole-bodily, with your whole experience. Never stop questioning. The further you question, the more you will know.

{ An idea that is developed and put into action is more important than an idea that exists only as an idea."
~ Siddhartha Gautama (The Buddha), 563–483 B.C. }

I had a friend say repeatedly that she should have known to give herself what she wanted. "I know this, I *know* this," she repeated as she continued berating herself.

"Not knowing is not the problem; and so knowing is not the solution," I said, "Doing is! You must do it."
(PS—How does "I should have known" feel, good or bad?)

{ Therefore, be ye lamps unto yourselves, be a refuge to yourselves. Hold fast to Truth as a lamp; hold fast to the truth as a refuge. Look not for a refuge in anyone beside yourselves. And those, who shall be a lamp unto themselves, shall betake themselves to no external refuge, but holding fast to the Truth as their lamp, and holding fast to the Truth as their refuge, they shall reach the topmost height.

~ Siddhartha Gautama (The Buddha), 563–483 B.C. }

CHAPTER 0

There Is No Such Thing as an Ending and Here We Are

After first writing this book, powerful new insights began to come. I stopped writing and continued helping people find their way out of painful mind traps. Then a book contest called "The Next Top Spiritual Author Contest" launched and spanned eight months. I took the time during the contest to reconsider the things I wrote, and how I wrote them, and in light of my new insights, I began "cleaning up" the book. The time of learning during the contest and of working with people and fine-tuning the practice and the questions made the book even better.

The message and practice had already helped over a thousand people, and I knew it was going to help a lot more people, win or lose the contest. In fact, there was never an idea of "win or lose," it was just a question of how the book was going to get out there, and I took action while I watched the contest unfold, with interest—and detachment. I never applied any of the "Laws of Attraction," and I never believed that it could not win.

We were to submit a book proposal that included a summary, the chapter outline, a marketing plan, and two chapters. The first cut was based on public votes, and I worked hard. Out of 2,800 books worldwide, *Alchemy* made the top 250. The second cut combined votes and a selection committee, and the book made the top twenty-five. After submitting another chapter, a panel of experts selected it for the top four. With each cut, I simply waited to see; waited to know if this was the direction the book was to continue taking, and what I was to do next, and with each cut my reaction was, "Oh, okay, this is the way it is going." I saw that everything was just happening, and there was no me doing it.

Finally the publisher who was awarding the book deal selected *The Alchemy of Love and Joy*™ as the winner. My strongest experience and response was not one of winning, but a knowing that a hurdle had been crossed, and that there was no turning back. It was affirmation that this book had value to readers *and* publishers. (With the feedback the last year, I already knew its value to readers.)

However when I received the contract, I was not moved to sign it. It seemed this was not the way the book would be published after all. Knowing that new authors rarely get offered *any* contract from a traditional publisher, the offer was not lightly dismissed. For two weeks I weighed all the pros and cons, and picked the brains of experts and authors. Until the decision made itself, until I knew which way the book was going, I did nothing. There was no personal attachment to winning, nor to the title of "Next Top Spiritual Author," and it was purely a business decision backed by intuition. I did not sign.

Many people were shocked; how could I not sign after all this? But I did not participate with attachment to the fruit of the outcome. Who am I to say what the outcome should be? There is an infinite universe at work, not separate from this. Any personal attachment is not necessarily what's best.

Many people warned me it was an error. But I know there are no errors. There are many different ways that books become successful, and not being attached, I was able to see and know clearly. There is no winning, there is no losing. There is no good, there is no bad. There is just what is. It was not about me, it was not about hope or desire; it was about the publishing offer and everything else that was available—it was about the context, the situation, and the ecology that this very book speaks about! The sense that there was not a "me" doing anything, remained. Everything continued to just unfold.

The people and connections the book needed fell into place on their own just before the win, and I learned and acquired everything required to professionally publish the book under my own imprint in order for it to be successful and to be of maximum benefit to people—except one thing. That final missing piece arrived at the last possible moment, while waiting to know what the decision was. Just as there is no me who won the contest, there was no me deciding not to sign. The decision finally made itself. Ultimately, not accepting was as big a win as accepting, and once again, I knew which way the book was going, *for now*—because as I am sure you now know, there is no ending.

There is more evidence of that here because the direct seeing in the woods almost made me throw the book out. It was that experience of the unspeakable that compelled me to strip away the concepts in the book. That was critical, and I felt that I could not clean it up enough.

Books appear to start and end, but like all illusions, that is just appearance. Although authors could edit perpetually, if I did not stop working on it at some point then you'd not be holding it at this moment. Now the torch is in your hands—don't *you* stop as the words stop in this book, because words are just thought, and as the experience in the woods taught me, thought is not *It*.

And yet we communicate with words. So my last words here encourage you to use thought and feeling, and not pretend to let them use you. That which knows thought cannot be contained *by* thought. Question everything you think you know; question all the questions until they burn themselves up, and return to the immaculate purity of not knowing, so that you can know That which cannot be thought, the Unspeakable.

The Alchemy of Love and Joy™

When you suffer, you are *wanting* something.
As soon as you feel any pain or discomfort, ask yourself,

"What do I want?" (instead)

Answer it positively, as what you *do* want: (write it below)

"How does _____(what I want) feel?"

How else does it feel? And how else?
Feel into your whole body as you do this, open your peripheral vision, feel your breath. Feel for the answer in and with your body. Take your time looking for "it," and when you "latch" onto "it," appreciate it. Words, images may arise and that is okay, but stay laser-focused on the good feeling. Keep enjoying it fully, appreciating it, every time it grows.

At the peak, ask yourself:

"Is this what I prefer to feel?" And then,

"Who's _____(what I want) did I need for this?"

Maintaining the good feeling, look back on or notice the outer circumstances or person.

"What do you think of it or them now?"

If your energy drops, start over and rebuild. Repeat this until you can maintain feeling good in the face of adversity.

When feeling peak good, notice the suffering option, and if you feel drawn into it, flip quickly back to feeling the joy. Do this repeatedly until you know you are the source, the cause, and the control of your attention direction, and of how you feel.

"Feeling this way, how do I act?"

"Is this what I prefer to do, share, give, or project?"

When you are feeling really good, acknowledge the circumstances that are, as they exist, unchanged. When you fully achieve this, there will be a sense of release followed by a deep sweetness that comes with re-alignment with truth of what is. Enjoy it. Then accept it with gratitude and appreciation. (You may notice some positive thoughts arising.)

Use suffering for the only thing it is good for—to point you toward joy.

Please, share *The Alchemy of Love and Joy*™ with everyone.

Free Audio, Video, TeleClasses and Other Resources:
http://www.AlchemyLoveJoy.com

We don't need to kill the non-existent ego.

We don't need to struggle with thoughts.

We don't need to work on the "past."

There is nothing to let go of.

We don't need the future.

So simple.

Simply embrace feeling what you *do* want.

You can awaken love and joy any time, any place.

It is always present, always available.

It is always you.

Love is Eternal.

Remember.
—Seek Joy!

Beyond Fireworks

When the desire to control my state sprang forth I did not know it would just be a side-trip. The real treasure was to realize that I am not my state. From that perspective, I can move attention off the state, in essence pulling the power plug.

There is a saying that when a thorn is embedded in the skin, you use another thorn to remove it and then *throw them both away*. Suffering is a gift in disguise that can be unwrapped in the moment to reveal treasure that cannot be measured. Using the desire to feel good, using *Alchemy*, is like using a thorn.

Use *Alchemy* for freedom from attachment, but beware seeking and attaching to a "final" state that is never changing and always happy. That is not what awakening is, and the effort goes against the very nature of experience, which must change in order for there to *be* experience.

I hesitated to speak about the Unspeakable because people seek these mystical states which can be mistaken for what they are not, and you can get stuck there. I have heard of people who have experienced peaceful, blissful, or ecstatic states, who made the mistake of thinking that the state was "It," and that they must "get it back." They say that "it left," or that they must "go back there," which of course implies that they went somewhere and returned—*but they never budged.*

They just mistook the *experience,* which comes and goes, for Self, which does not, clinging to what was merely an experience, already past and gone. It cannot "leave," and there is no place to "get back" to. These are concepts, ideas which, themselves, believed in, appear to keep people from It.

The "fireworks" of truth can be very impressive and distracting, but *who is it that knows the fireworks?* Which is greater? The fireworks which come and go, or The Eternal Witness of coming and going? You are not the fireworks, the fireworks are not It.

There is an ancient story about a man who was sentenced to be beheaded who suffered, waiting, for months before. The final day before the dreaded event, he had a blissful glimpse of truth, and looked forward to the execution. But at the last minute, he was pardoned and released. Two years later, he died an alcoholic, having spent the next two years trying to "get back there."

Suffering did not lead to direct seeing of Self, nor did a joyful state either. These were experiences, and no experience can elicit direct seeing. There was calm, concentration, mindfulness (presence), joy, equanimity, energy, and a new piece: investigative questioning into what I thought I knew. (More details on this in my blog).

Seeking experiences in the spirit of growth or self-improvement of the separated sense of "I," you are looking in the wrong direction. The experience is not the cause of seeing the Divine, or the Self; the experience *is the result* of such seeing.

Like you cannot become a Buddha or Jesus through effort, the "I" cannot mimic or concoct the fireworks experience in hopes of causing awakening. The "I" cannot be awakened. The dissolution or collapse of the "I," of false knowledge of self and other, of separation, is the dropping of the veil of belief to reveal what was always already the case.

Use *Alchemy* to release yourself from the pain of attachment to what changes, but do not seek or attach to states of bliss or ecstasy themselves. It's the difference between temporary joy (which can be a trap or a tool), and eternal joy and freedom. Seek only the Divine, or to know who or what you really are, because it is said that when you seek the Divine, you find yourself, and when you seek yourself, you find the Divine.

There. Is. No. Separation.

CINDY TEEVENS

About the Author

The simple and powerful practice of *Alchemy* came through her own suffering and later discovery of joy, and it emerged and took form in words, to help someone else. Her life has become happy and often ecstatic with the simplest of things. Filled with gratitude and unable to contain what happened, she was compelled to drop everything and write *Alchemy*. Prior to that she was a print and web publisher and now she gives talks, facilitates workshops and retreats, gives private sessions, and encourages everyone to—*seek joy!*

Cindy resides in Ottawa, Canada.

More stories, her blog, and audio recordings can be accessed at: http://www.AlchemyLoveJoy.com

Dear Reader,

Hopefully you will not be satisfied with merely reading this book. That would be a good thing because only by doing the practice, only by actualizing it and seeking joy in the power of now can you turn your world around.

I lead groups, individuals, and couples through programs that are based on the book and the practice of *Alchemy*. Visit the website for more information and dates on:

- ❑ Free Webinars
- ❑ Retreats
- ❑ Couples Programs
- ❑ Memberships, Community Forum
- ❑ Free Video, Audio Access

http://www.AlchemyLoveJoy.com

Thank you for reading, being curious about this world with a fresh new view, and being okay with not being certain—it is after all, the only place where other possibilities lie.

Peace of Being,

Cindy

PS—Bonus Resources:
http://www.egoidkit.com <--Free Ego I.D. Kit Download
http://www.edgeouttheego.com <--Free Ego Videos

9 780981 376301